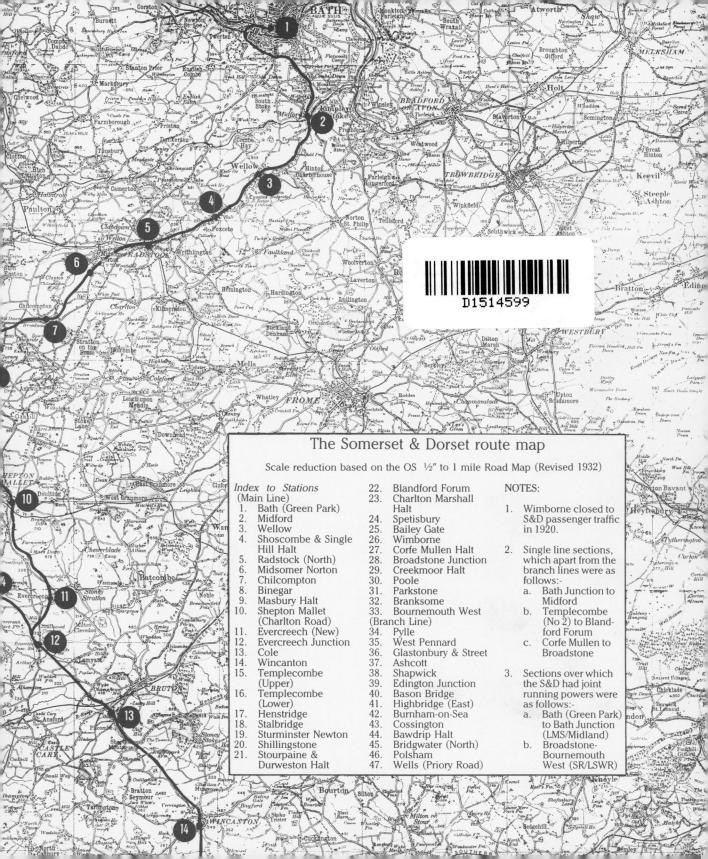

D1514599

The Somerset & Dorset route map

Scale reduction based on the OS ½″ to 1 mile Road Map (Revised 1932)

Index to Stations
(Main Line)

1. Bath (Green Park)
2. Midford
3. Wellow
4. Shoscombe & Single Hill Halt
5. Radstock (North)
6. Midsomer Norton
7. Chilcompton
8. Binegar
9. Masbury Halt
10. Shepton Mallet (Charlton Road)
11. Evercreech (New)
12. Evercreech Junction
13. Cole
14. Wincanton
15. Templecombe (Upper)
16. Templecombe (Lower)
17. Henstridge
18. Stalbridge
19. Sturminster Newton
20. Shillingstone
21. Stourpaine & Durweston Halt
22. Blandford Forum
23. Charlton Marshall Halt
24. Spetisbury
25. Bailey Gate
26. Wimborne
27. Corfe Mullen Halt
28. Broadstone Junction
29. Creekmoor Halt
30. Poole
31. Parkstone
32. Branksome
33. Bournemouth West

(Branch Line)

34. Pylle
35. West Pennard
36. Glastonbury & Street
37. Ashcott
38. Shapwick
39. Edington Junction
40. Bason Bridge
41. Highbridge (East)
42. Burnham-on-Sea
43. Cossington
44. Bawdrip Halt
45. Bridgwater (North)
46. Polsham
47. Wells (Priory Road)

NOTES:

1. Wimborne closed to S&D passenger traffic in 1920.

2. Single line sections, which apart from the branch lines were as follows:-
   a. Bath Junction to Midford
   b. Templecombe (No 2) to Blandford Forum
   c. Corfe Mullen to Broadstone

3. Sections over which the S&D had joint running powers were as follows:-
   a. Bath (Green Park) to Bath Junction (LMS/Midland)
   b. Broadstone-Bournemouth West (SR/LSWR)

THE
SOMERSET
&
DORSET
THEN AND NOW

THE SOMERSET & DORSET THEN AND NOW

Mac Hawkins

Patrick Stephens, Wellingborough

The author and publishers have made every effort to
ensure that the 'then & now' photographs are exact
facsimiles. Due to normal production and printing
practices, certain details may have been 'bled off' by the
binding or trimming of this book.

The differences will be minor and therefore it is hoped
that they do not detract from the accuracy that this
publication endeavours to achieve.

First published in 1986
Reprinted February 1987

British Library Cataloguing in Publication Data

Hawkins, Mac
    The Somerset & Dorset: then and now.
    1. Somerset & Dorset Joint Railway – History
    I. Title
    385'.09423   HE3020.S6

    ISBN 0-85059-797-8

Patrick Stephens Limited is part of the
Thorsons Publishing Group

Printed and bound in Great Britain.

Contents

Foreword   6

Preface   7

Some Background Notes   9

Chapter   1   Bath – Devonshire Tunnel   11

Chapter   2   Lyncombe Vale – Midford Valley   27

Chapter   3   Wellow – Radstock   43

Chapter   4   Midsomer Norton – Binegar   62

Chapter   5   Masbury – Winsor Hill   81

Chapter   6   Shepton Mallet – Evercreech   101

Chapter   7   Wyke Champflower – Wincanton   128

Chapter   8   Templecombe – Stourpaine and Durweston   150

Chapter   9   Blandford Forum – Bournemouth   173

Chapter 10   Pylle – Edington Junction   196

Chapter 11   Bason Bridge – Burnham-on-Sea   220

Chapter 12   Bridgwater and Wells Branches   239

Appendices   254

Foreword

by Peter Smith

When Dr Beeching's figurative axe fell, as it did repeatedly during the 1960s, it left not only many parts of the British Isles remote from a railway line, but it also resulted in a substantial reduction in the number of jobs available for railwaymen.

Even before the '50s were out, the high cost of its operation, together with the dramatic increase in private motoring, made it almost a foregone conclusion that the ex-Somerset & Dorset Joint Railway – on which I was an engineman for ten years—would not escape the purge, though it was no less traumatic for those involved when the end finally did come on 6 March 1966.

As one who left the services of BR in November 1963 as a combined result of the impending closure of the S&D and the gradual demise of steam traction on the Southern Region, I, like many of my colleagues, had for some years after, no wish to go back and view the torn-up remnants of a route I once knew so well, and of which I had so many happy memories. However, time heals: in recent years I have frequently found myself thinking, 'I wonder what the old line looks like now?'

Certainly my activities in recent years, recalling on paper, tape recorder and film, memories of this once fascinating railway, have provided some incentive to revisit several locations—particularly at the northern end of the line in connection with the recent BBC television programme, 'Return to Evercreech Junction', but much remained unvisited. Some of this new-found curiosity was satisfied during the early summer of 1985 when Mac Hawkins contacted me whilst researching this book. Thereafter we visited together a number of locations south of Templecombe and I grew more and more fascinated as I began to appreciate what he was trying to achieve—and, of course, the memories came flooding back.

Happily the S&D scene was copiously recorded on film by a number of excellent photographers over the years. Notable amongst these is my old friend, Ivo Peters, whose frequency of appearance by the line side was such that his face was as familiar to most engine crews as, say, Midford up outer home signal!

Now, utilizing skills acquired as a one-time carto-grapher, combined with his considerable ability as a photographer, Mac Hawkins has carefully surveyed the present S&D scenario. With the aid of suitable photographs taken by Ivo and his contemporaries, depicting the S&D at its zenith, he has here brought a new dimension to the well-known 'Then & Now' theme of environmental change through the years, as portrayed by the photographer and his camera.

Following—almost literally—in Ivo's footsteps, Mac and I have clambered up embankments and fought our way through overgrown and fly-ridden cuttings: I should point out that my friend Mike Arlett has been similarly engaged with Mac on the northern half of the line. I have watched with a mixture of amusement and amazement the intrepid and painstaking Mac, perched perilously on a wooden pallet, being hoisted by a mechanical digger twenty or more feet into the air in order to obtain a facsimile photograph at a spot where once stood a convenient footbridge or signal post to assist previous photographers of the line.

The end result for those who are not able, or who do not wish to get involved in the physical difficulty of walking what track-bed is still available (but who find themselves thinking from time to time, 'I wonder what the old line looks like now,') is this admirable volume. Even non-railway enthusiasts will find much to ponder as they view the changes forced on the environment—whether for good or ill depends very much on one's point of view—by market forces and progress. It all adds yet another facet to the treasured memories and chequered history of the never-to-be-forgotten Somerset and Dorset Joint Railway.

Peter Smith
July 1985

Peter Smith, the author of *Mendips Engineman* and *Footplate over the Mendips*, drove the last 'Up' 'Pines Express' hauled by Standard Class '9F' No 92220, *Evening Star*, on 8 September 1962.

Preface

Whilst the S&D was being run down and the railway system throughout Britain undergoing dramatic changes, I was blissfully unaware of these events!

I have always had a strong love of trains and living in Devon from 1949–59 and going to school in Sussex meant that I travelled a fair amount by train. The journeys to school seemed dreadful affairs, catching the 10.00 hours from Exeter St David's to Paddington and then going across London and travelling from Victoria to Horsham. The engine appeared to be working uphill all the way to Paddington and with brakes applied, such was my reluctance to make the journey! However, on the return trip at holiday times my feelings were very different—the mercurial flight west behind a 'King' or a 'Castle' would set my pulse racing.

Having had an eye for aesthetics from an early age, I can remember with horror the first sight of a 'Castle' fitted with a double chimney. 'What a dreadful thing to do to such a fine looking engine!' I thought. I can remember too the short footplate ride on my favourite engine, No 4073, *Caerphilly Castle*, at Exeter St Davids and also on the Moretonhampstead branch—a chance to 'run round' the train on the footplate of a '45XX' 2-6-2T.

By good fortune my school happened to be on the Victoria to Portsmouth line at Christ's Hospital, whose station then boasted seven platforms and formed the junction with the Horsham to Guildford branch. The trains from Horsham to Shoreham via Itchingfield Junction also used to pass through here. Although not exciting by steam enthusiasts' standards, the line still provided welcome relief from the insoluble problems of Pythagoras and Newton! The sight of a 'C2X' struggling with an 'Up' goods past Itchingfield Junction was fairly common, as were the M7 Motor Tanks with their Auto trains – affectionately known to us as the 'Brighton Slacker' or the 'Guildford Slacker'. The excitement of seeing an occasional Bo-Bo or, even, Co-Co, would break the monotony of the 'fast' and 'slow' electric sets used on that line! But nothing really matched the Great Western in my eyes—which longed to see a haughty 'Castle' surrounded by chocolate and cream.

I left school in 1960 and shortly afterwards I joined the Army and trained as a topographical surveyor. Two short tours in the Far East during the Indonesian Confrontation took me through to the mid '60s. My interest in aviation was an abiding one and therefore the run-down of steam went almost unnoticed, I am ashamed to say. On leaving the Army in 1965 and joining a large tobacco company that year, I was left very little time or opportunity to follow every interest.

My connection with the Somerset & Dorset was tenuous to say the least. I can remember seeing Collett 0-6-0s waiting in the station at Highbridge (East) whilst I was being hauled towards Nottingham behind a 'Warship'. I did actually travel on the Bridgwater Branch as a boy, to my regret my only chance to sample at first hand the line's charm, although I was not old enough to appreciate it.

Over the years my topographical training and interest in old railways has often meant my long-suffering family or a colleague having to endure a broken car journey in order that I could clamber up some embankment to look at an old line formation, or peer over a bridge to see derelict platforms of a once-proud station. My amazement as to how so much human endeavour and resource could end this way has never been satisfactorily answered.

One Christmas I was given Robin Atthill's fine book *The Somerset & Dorset Railway* – and I got the bug – later fed further by Ivo Peters' first book on the S&D *The Somerset & Dorset—An English Cross Country Railway*. This ensured that my interest in the S&D railway line was well and truly in the blood. I had previously visited Shepton Mallet in 1967 and photographed a diesel-hauled demolition train coming over the Charlton Road Viaduct on its way down the line. Over the years I was able to pay my respects to the S&D as well as other lines around the country, to see how a scene could change in a relatively short passage of time.

In 1982 I became self-employed and had the chance to utilize cartographic skills acquired some twenty years previously in the Army, together with my interest in photography, which had been directed towards aviation. These two interests happen to combine well and I began to think that they could be put to good use in a way which would add a new dimension to the railway scene. I am the first one to confess that the precise details of running a railway have eluded me to a greater degree! The fact of whether the train was the 13.10 'Up' or the 16.13 'Down' was of no great concern to me! So I bow to the extent of knowledge that experts acquire and to the infinite enjoyment they gain from such. To me the sight and smell of a steam engine passing through gorgeous countryside is reward enough and is something that I will always remember and treasure.

A further four S&D volumes from Ivo Peters convinced me that I should 'go/see'. Over the next year or so and with a lot of planning I was able to produce a synopsis for the publisher. Late in 1984 the green light or rather the semaphore signal 'off' was given, and these plans were put into action. The logistics of collecting suitable material in order to provide such a study were simply horrendous. I could write a book on that alone! However, suffice to say that I contacted some of the leading experts on the S&D and it has been my good fortune to have made friends with many charming people in the process, without whose help this book could not have been made possible.

In an attempt to meet publishers' deadlines a planned six months' work was compacted to three in the spring and summer of 1985 spent photographing the line—that was the easy part! I thoroughly enjoyed meeting many more delightful people in the process who were always ready to help in any way they could. I also enjoyed tremendously the company of my friends Mike Arlett and Peter Smith, both of whom accompanied me on forays up and down the line and whose friendly banter kept me going—sometimes in the face of adversity (particularly the weather!) – I regret to say that welcome visits to a hostelry were seldom made before 14.00 hours because of my insistence on 'Just one more shot to take, then we'll go!'

I have tried to select photographs, both for their content and their quality, and have endeavoured to add as many as possible that have not previously been published. I make no apology for including others that have, particularly those of Ivo Peters, whose photographs are superb and provided me with the content and composition that perfectly summarizes all that I find so interesting in steam; they also provide a tangible link with a once familiar scene. Some of my favourite photographs have been impossible to reproduce because of Mother Nature's insistent restaking of her claim.

I hope the end result is of interest to many, including S&D 'buffs'. I should like to dedicate this volume to all the ex-S & D staff who gave so much of their lives to this wonderful line.

Some background notes

The date of 6 March 1966 was a day of infamy in many people's eyes when trains ran over one of the country's best loved railways for the last time. The Somerset & Dorset line, which ran for 71½ miles from Bath to Bournemouth, over the lovely Mendip Hills in Somerset and through some of the best country with which the County of Dorset has been blessed, closed to traffic for ever from Monday 7 March.

The penetrating line of the Somerset & Dorset had been controlled by the Western Region since 1958—thereafter, a few people thought it was bound to be doomed. Through passenger traffic was diverted from the line in 1962, thus depriving the system of its life's blood. Together with the gradual process of re-routing freight traffic, particularly from the North Cornwall lines, which had greatly contributed to its revenue over the years, along with coal from the Somerset Coalfields and Mendip stone, the line's demise was underway. The coalfields were already suffering from the availability of cheaper alternatives such as oil and, ironically, were failing to attract sufficient labour to work in the pits, thus reducing potential output, and thus hastening final closure of both line and mine (the last mine closed in 1973).

Much blame has been apportioned to the Western Region for the S&D's demise. A census of passenger traffic was taken during school holidays (when traffic was considerably less), and '9F' engines instead of the requested Class '5MT's were sent in 1963 to work local passenger services, to highlight just two cited examples of Western Region disinterest. However, even taking all these factors into account and with the benefit of hind-sight, the line probably would not have survived the 'Beeching Axe' in any event.

Beeching's Report of 28 March 1963 entitled *The Reshaping of British Railways* argued that a third of the system should be axed. Fares would rise to compensate for the loss of capacity. The report envisaged that 75 per cent of the population would have a car by 1984 (now proven to be over optimistic). It was true that the country was becoming more wealthy—the 'you've never had it so good' era had hardly begun! People were discovering the freedom that the motor car offered and at home the washing was being done with the aid of one of John Bloom's machines. Even summer rail traffic was getting less and less. The railways had already embarked upon a massive dieselization programme by 1966, resulting in steam engines of less than ten years of age being scrapped, engines that were still good for another 500,000 miles or more and the type of motive power upon which the S&D still totally depended.

It is now generally accepted that the Beeching Report was a crude cost-cutting exercise and as somebody pointed out 'If you cut the tributaries of a river you are depriving it of the sources upon which it depends'. It is an irony that twenty years or more since the sharpness of the axe was felt, stations closed then are beginning to re-open around the country. Templecombe is but one example – and it is earning *good* revenue!

The railways of Britain are a marvellous asset which the confident Victorians bequeathed to us. If engineers were to sit down today, given a blank sheet of paper and asked to design a mass transport system, I wonder how many times 'railway system' would be their answer?

The other vital point which many statisticians and economists seem to constantly underestimate, is the human factor. The Beeching Report meant that some 70,000 people would lose their jobs: many would be of retiring age it is true, and the job shortage was not as acute as it is today, but it obviously had a totally de-moralizing effect on many.

It took generations of men to build up and run a railway – it did not happen overnight – and to a great degree its success depended on the people that ran it. The conditions of work, in some cases, certainly, were not to be desired and the pay was very meagre. Even after a lifetime's devoted duty, a top link driver in the early 1960s could not expect to earn more than £10/12 per week—hardly a handsome reward for his service and responsibilities. Despite this, many railwaymen seemed to carve out a good quality of life for themselves, however simple by today's standards, and this was often to be reflected in the way the S&D stations and gardens were kept, the beautiful flowerbeds and productive allotments which were a joy for passengers to behold. This apparent contentment with life is to be envied in today's world full of hatred and greed.

Therefore it was often a special *esprit de corps* that railway men had, none more so than the men on the Somerset & Dorset, which epitomized this quality. Undoubtedly there were a few people on the S&D who were known to be a little 'peppery', to say the least, and who did not necessarily fit into the mould of that 'nice kind helpful railwayman' image! It is a common practice, especially where steam engines are concerned, for enthusiasts and historians to look through rose-coloured spectacles when viewing the railway scenario after the era has long since disappeared. Images tend to get a little distorted but nevertheless the S&D was something special.

By the winter of 1962 the S&D had resorted to a local service. Anomalies had crept in with connecting services still being run, like the Down stopping train, 16.13 from Evercreech – with no train to meet, and run from a place where there was nobody to use it. Like many of the stations on the line, Evercreech served a scattered, predominantly agricultural population, who just did not use the system, except nearer to Bath. As a railway operating services for this kind of community, apart from school traffic and the occasional excursion, it could not be expected to pay and survive.

The need for double-headed operation on heavy trains on the ruling 1:50 gradient over the Mendips played an important factor in diverting traffic from the line, particularly because of the extra manpower needed in order to operate this service. The arrival of the Standard Class '9F' 2-10-0s on the scene in the summer of 1960 following a trial in the March of that year, was hailed as a saviour by some, but seen as a threat by others. The unions were very chary about the possible reduction in manpower that the introduction of these magnificent engines would bring about. This fear was somewhat unfounded for although these powerful locomotives could haul 450

tons over the Mendips unassisted, it was an onerous task for the firemen of such trains to keep their drivers supplied with a sustained full head of steam in order to do so! Therefore in practical terms such trains continued to be double headed – back to square one! There was an interesting suggestion of rostering two firemen per '9F' on such trains, but for various reasons this proposal was not followed through.

So, eventually, the 'Pines Express' would no more traverse the line. Evercreech Junction on Saturday mornings, a mecca for steam enthusiasts, would not see the sight of five pilot engines waiting in the centre siding between the platforms to assist trains over the Mendips. The variety of motive power that attracted the many enthusiasts to the line would diminish to a degree, but not to the extent that it was boring—for that it never was! The Somerset & Dorset lingered on until March 1966, reprieved by two months due to a bus operator withdrawing an application for a licence. Valiant attempts to save the line were made by various bodies. Two stalwarts of the S&D who played a leading part in trying to bring about a reprieve were Norman Down, the station master of Binegar, and Ernie Cross, the signalman. To the shame of the railway authorities and the Labour government of the day, this came to nothing. So the S&D passed into history, 104 years after its formation.

Today, two decades after closure, the remains of this beautiful line are still deeply impressed upon the landscape in many areas. Other parts have totally reverted back to their original use or have been built upon and nothing remains. It is ironic that some artefacts are in better condition today than they were in railway days, namely Bath Green Park Station and Charlton Viaduct at Shepton Mallet.

So let us remind ourselves of what the S&D was like with the aid of some splendid photographs taken during its last few decades and compare the same scenes today – The Somerset & Dorset 'Then & Now'.

Chapter 1
Bath – Devonshire Tunnel

1

Bath Green Park Station façade (172 ST 746 648)

A 1959 view of the façade taken in railway days—a noble structure built of Bath Stone in Georgian style. Like many buildings of the period it was in need of a good clean. *(Photo: R. C. Riley. Date: 5 July 1959.)*

Restored to its former glory—its stonework repaired and cleaned like a new pin, the station façade forms the pedestrian entrance to J. Sainsbury's supermarket. The ground floor houses a café and lobby area whilst the large first floor room, whose windows are draped with curtains, is used by The Bath Society. This photograph was taken on the same date 26 years later! *(Date: 5 July 1985.)*

Note: map references are given for the 1:50,000 OS Landranger Series, and represent the point from which the photographs were taken.

Map 1 1932: Bath Green Park

It has been stated that the station opened as the terminus of the Midland Railway's branch line from Mangotsfield on 7 May 1870, a temporary station being used on the west side of the river upon the line's opening on 4 August 1869. Research has now shown that, although far from complete, the station was in fact used right from the date that the line opened.

The station, unofficially named as 'Queen Square' (it was to remain as such until nationalization) was built at the junction of James Street West, Charles Street, Green Park/Seymour Street. The façade was appropriately built in Bath stone and was of Georgian appearance. The train shed had an overall glazed roof covering half of the platform length. There were four lines into the station, but only the outer two had platform faces.

The station welcomed a new visitor on 20 July 1874 when the S&D's Bath extension was opened, joining the Midland Railway at Bath Junction, half a mile or so due west of the terminus. Gradual development occurred in Bath over the next few years and by the turn of the century the railways had in essence achieved their final form.

The 1932 layout differed little from that at the time of the closure of the S&D apart from around the shed areas. The area between the large engine shed (S&D) and Victoria Bridge Road was altered to incorporate a water softening plant and just post-war two oil storage tanks were added, only to be demolished in the '50s. In the mid '30s a 60ft turntable was provided nearer the Midland shed.

The two engine sheds are clearly visible on the map – the larger being the S&D shed, which was built mainly of wood and asbestos, having four roads, enabling eighteen engines to be accommodated. The Midland Railway's shed is the

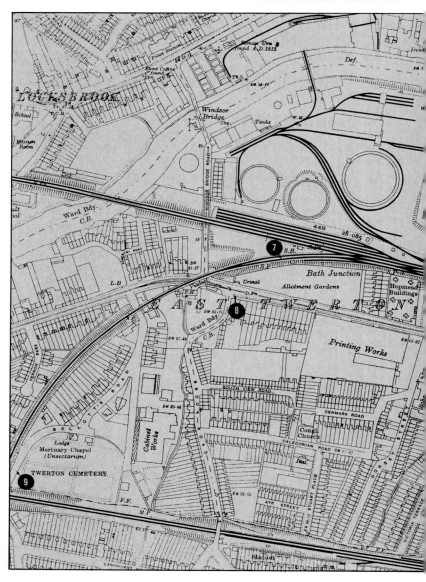

smaller, built of stone and of far more solid construction. It had two roads and from 1935 access was gained over a 60ft turntable.

The station platforms were never adequate to accommodate the twelve-coach summer expresses. The northern platform could take eight bogie coaches and the southern nine. It was obviously impractical to extend them for this

purpose, as the station was hemmed in to the west by the River Avon, over which two parallel and costly iron girder bridges were built to carry the railway.

Three gasometers near the site of Bath Junction still stand out as a landmark today, as they did then. The bridges over Midland Road and Victoria Bridge Road have since been removed.

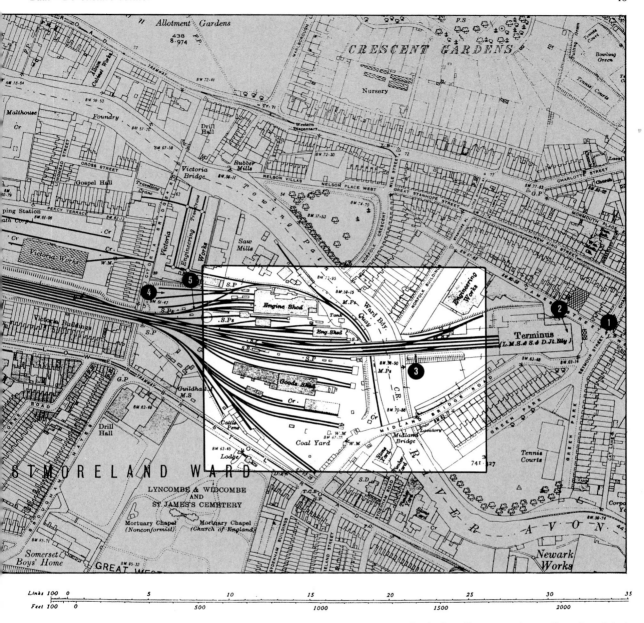

Scale for all maps unless otherwise stated

Boxed area above indicates the area covered by Map 2.

Numbers on maps refer to photographs appearing within these pages.

Map 2 1985: Bath Green Park

The area marked on Map 1 is covered by this map. The changes are all too obvious. Sainsbury's supermarket is situated just east of the River Avon and nestles up to the old train shed, now beautifully restored. One bridge (northern side) has been replaced with a modern pedestrian version, which allows access from the car park located on the west bank of the river. A small industrial estate now occupies the site of the goods yard. The scrap yard shown on the map has now been cleared and is to be developed by Sainsbury's as a DIY centre. The road names provide a poignant reminder of the area's railway history, with appellations such as 'Pines Way', 'Stanier Road', 'Beale Road', and also, after a famous son of Bath, 'Ivo Peters Road'.

2
Bath Green Park train shed
(177 ST 745 648)

Drivers Dave Hadfield and Bert Brewer bring their respective charges '2P' No 40563 and BR Class '5' No 73050 slowly to a halt at the buffer stops on the 'Up' 'Pines Express'. Note the familiar advertising hoardings of the period and the war-damaged roof remaining unglazed. *(Photo: Ivo Peters. Date: 3 July 1954.)*

In April 1942 Bath was the target for one of the notorious Baedeker reprisal raids, carried out on historic towns and cities throughout the country. The building caught the blast of the first bomb dropped on the city during the raid in which the old S&D offices in Green Park Buildings were destroyed.

After closure of the line in 1966,

the station began to deteriorate rapidly, the buildings suffered considerable damage and decay, not helped by the roof lead being stolen. In November 1971 it was made a listed building and in 1972 Bath City Council decided to purchase the site. A number of repairs were then effected, to prevent further decay.

During the next seven years various schemes for development were mooted, the council expressing a preference for a hotel to be built, which would have meant the train shed being demolished. Then in October 1979 Bath City Council gave official support to enter into an agreement between the British Railways Board and J. Sainsbury to the leasing of the site (with planning permission) for the erection of a retail store which included the restoration of the station building.

Late in 1979 structural surveys

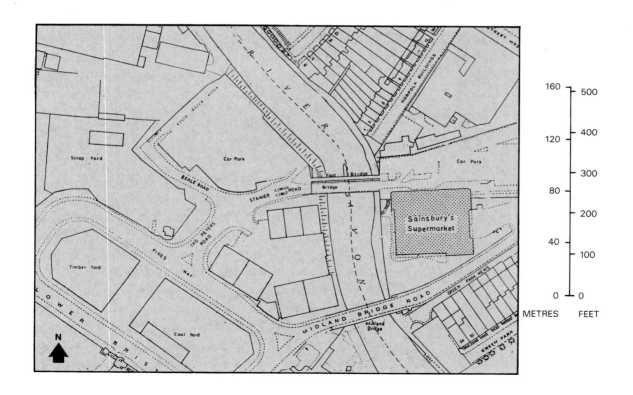

were carried out, which revealed the desperate condition of the building. However, restoration commenced in earnest in 1981 and involved many complex engineering and construction techniques to ensure that the essential character and appearance of the building remained. After some £1,500,000 and 44 weeks spent on restoration Green Park was formally opened by HRH Princess Margaret on 1 December 1982. The building today reflects a magnificent achievement by all concerned.

The train shed, now beautifully restored and protected by a glazed roof, stands empty in the evening light after the last shoppers have left. The supermarket is seen in the background. Note the recently paved area that once formed the track-bed adjacent to the buffer stops.

The station rooms have been let to a variety of businesses, including the Green Park Café (specializing in health type foods), paper making and printing, dress designer shop, building society office, hand painted pine furniture, Bath Enterprises (small industries group) and upstairs, the meeting room of The Bath Society. *(Date: 14 June 1985.)*

3
Bath Green Park Station
(172 ST 744 647)

The 10.10 local to Bristol Temple Meads, hauled by 'Peak' type 4 diesel No D 12, receives admiring glances as BR Class '5' 4-6-0 No 73164 surefootedly gets under way with the 09.55 semi-fast for Bournemouth West. (*Photo: Ivo Peters. Date: 24 September 1963.*)

Two evening shoppers get to grips with the meanderings of a super-market trolley! Standing serenely in the background, the train shed, looking majestic, watches over its new patrons. Sainsbury's store can just be seen on the right of the picture. Trees have been planted in the car parks and access here is via one of the original railway bridges spanning the River Avon, to the north side of which a new ped-estrian bridge has been con-structed, using the abutments of its demolished twin. Green Park will no more be host to steam trains, but it stands as a worthy monument to them, the best possible alternative use being made of it, and it looks simply magnificent! *(Date: 24 June 1985.)*

4
Bath sheds (172 ST 741 648)

A fine study of Bath MPD taken from the top of the old water treatment plant set between the sheds and Victoria Bridge Road. Taken a few months before through summer traffic on the S&D was diverted, the scene shows considerable activity, with a bevy of Stanier Class '5' 4-6-0s, including numbers 44666, 44775, 44888, 44804 and 44667, together with two '9F' 2-10-0s, numbers 92210 and 92001 in evidence.

Note the reporting number being placed on the smoke box of '9F' 92210, also locomen 'chewing the fat' outside the dry sand bin. Green Park Station building can be seen in the middle distance as can some of Bath's many church spires and Bath Abbey.

The S&D wooden shed in the foreground could house eighteen locomotives, the smaller Midland stone-built shed is seen behind the coaling plant which itself was re-built in 1954. *(Photo: Ivo Peters. Date: 14 July 1962.)*

What a contrast! This photograph, taken from approximately the same spot, was made possible by the kind co-operation of Messrs Stothert & Pitt of Bath, who owned the site. They arranged for a large crane to be sited near to the spot where once stood the water treatment plant and with my helper, John Porter of Stothert's, I embarked upon an upward journey, seemingly to shake hands with the Almighty—but under the comfort of an umbrella which John kindly held over the camera equipment! The weather was atrocious, raining torrents—one could hardly see the hills in the background—but the magic of a uv filter fixed to the lens managed to penetrate the murk just enough to see the horizon.

A good idea of how Sainsbury's supermarket fits into the scene can be judged from this photograph. The land upon which the old S&D shed once stood is to be developed by them into a DIY store. Note the old retaining wall of the coaling stage still visible, the building adjacent to which uses the south wall to form part of its structure.

Insert The crane and cage in which I was lifted. *(Date: 21 May 1985.)*

5
Bath MPD (S & D shed)
(172 ST 742 648)

Locomotives on parade! The line-up includes S&D '7F' 2-8-0 53807, BR '9F' 2-10-0 92245, BR Class '4' 4-6-0 No 75073 and BR '9F' 2-10-0 No 92220, *Evening Star*, sporting the headboard of the line's premier train 'The Pines Express'. The climb from the S&D shed to the main line was sharp, but short, being set at a slightly lower level, causing some engines to do a bit of 'running on the spot' on the slippery rails in wet weather! *(Photo: Ivo Peters. Date: 8 September 1962.)*

Note the coaling stage retaining wall visible behind the black rubber screen today. Heavy plant built by Stothert & Pitt now replaces the Swindon, Derby and Darlington-built heavy machinery of 'Then' that once stood on this spot. *(Date: 17 June 1985.)*

6
Bath Junction and gasworks
(172 ST 738 648)

BR Class '5' 4-6-0 No 73050 drifts down the S&D single line past Bath Junction Signal Box with a rake of 'blood and custard' stock on the 'Up' 'Pines' relief. The gasometers at this point provide a landmark at the Junction with the Midland line to Mangotsfield and the north, which can be seen heading into the distance. *(Photo: Ivo Peters. Date: 23 April 1955.)*

The gasometers provide a tangible link, as do the houses in the distance. Note the new industrial development that has taken place on the site of the junction. The modern building shown in the 1955 picture has been demolished only thirty years later although the end of it is still visible. The photograph was taken from the site of a bracket signal just west of Midland Road. *(Date: 17 June 1985.)*

7
Bath Junction Signal Box
(172 ST 736 649)

All 'Down' trains had to collect the
tablet for the single line working to
Midford. Notice the catching
apparatus to the right of the picture.
Nearly all S&D engines were fitted
with a mechanical tablet catcher;
those that were not collected a 'big
pouch' tablet with a large metal
hoop which the signalman handed
to the fireman of such engines. Note
the Victoria Works in the background of Messrs Stothert & Pitt.
*(Photo: R. E. Toop. Date: 6 March
1966.)*

This photograph was taken on a
miserable day from the roof of a
lavatory belonging to an industrial
unit that has been built near the
site. The gasometers can just be
seen, to provide a reference point,
as can the Victoria Works. The
track-bed is used by a local garage
as a compound for new and used
cars. *(Date: 13 May 1985.)*

8
Lower Bristol Road, Bath
(172 ST 735 648)

BR Class '4' 2-6-0 No 76007 trundles over the Lower Bristol Road Bridge on her way down the line to beyond Midsomer Norton to do some engineering work. I wonder if the Advertising Standards people – if operating then – would have questioned the slogan under the S&D's bridge! Note the man in his 'Sunday Best' cycling along the deserted road, also 'The Royal Oak' public house. *(Photo: Ivo Peters. Date: 5 May 1957.)*

The only reminder today is 'The Royal Oak' public house. Even the houses across the road have made way for industrial development. The traffic would seem to suggest it *would* be quicker by train! *(Date: 13 May 1985.)*

9
Bath—Bellotts Road
(172 ST 733 646)

The assault on the 1:50 climb from Bath Junction has begun—the line curved through almost 180° and headed out of the city in a south-easterly direction. About half-way round this curve, the S&D passed over the GWR Paddington—Bristol main line, which Standard Class '5', 4-6-0 No 73047 is about to traverse with a 'Down' freight. *(Photo: R. E. Toop. Date: 13 October 1961.)*

The line has now become part of a linear way, which starts near this point. The embankment has gone, but little else has changed in this scene. Note the monument on the hill in the distance, which is known as Beckford's Tower. *(Date: 17 June 1985.)*

10
Devonshire Bank
(172 ST 743 636)

Having rounded the long curve from Bath Junction, BR Class '9F' 2-10-0 No 92001 storms up the 1:50 bank and under Maple Grove pedestrian bridge with the 07.43 (SO) Bradford to Bournemouth and on to Devonshire Tunnel, whose bore was very restricted and gave a clearance of under a foot from the chimney of some engines. The tunnel was ¼ mile long and had no ventilation shafts, making it extremely unpleasant for engine crews, particularly on the second engine of a double-headed train. *(Photo: Ivo Peters. Date: 14 July 1962.)*

The Devonshire Bank, now part of a linear park, has been landscaped, including slight backfilling of the cutting from Devonshire Tunnel. The footbridge across the track-bed is still visible, although in poor condition.
(Date: 17 June 1985.)
Insert A view looking west and down the linear way from on top of Devonshire Tunnel, the cap of which can be seen in the lower foreground. *(Date: 17 June 1985.)*

11
Devonshire Tunnel (172 ST 748 635)

S&D Class '7F' 2-8-0 No 53809 bursts out of Devonshire Tunnel with a 'Down' goods into Lyncombe Vale. The fireman leans out of the cab to fill his lungs with much needed fresh air after the stifling conditions experienced in the tunnel. *(Photo: Ivo Peters. Date: 15 March 1952.)*

The mouth of the tunnel has concrete blocks to fill all but a small portion of the portal. A good hour's pruning had to be undertaken before this view could be obtained. Note the telegraph pole that can just be seen on the right, which appears in the original. Unfortunately this area smelled of open drains and was very untidy despite the lovely lighting effect achieved in the photograph! *(Date: 14 June 1985.)*

Chapter 2
Lyncombe Vale—
Midford Valley

Map 3, 1904: Lyncombe Vale

The line emerged from Devonshire Tunnel and passed through this wooded vale for 30 chains at 1:50 before entering Combe Down Tunnel.

It is hard to imagine such a beautiful and secluded area as this is under a mile from the city centre, as the crow flies. The track-bed today is obscured by trees, although one can still walk along it between the two tunnels, with little difficulty. The two viaducts and the pedestrian overbridge survive, only the small under-bridge just east of Devonshire Tunnel has been demolished.

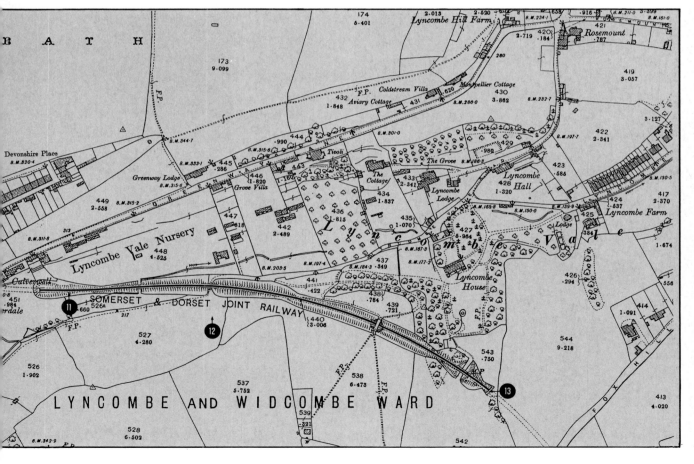

12
Lyncombe Vale (Watery Bottom Viaduct)
(172 ST 750 634)

An afternoon train to Bournemouth is hauled up the 1:50 climb towards Combe Down Tunnel over Watery Bottom Viaduct in the centre of Lyncombe Vale, by BR Class '4MT' 2-6-4(T) No 80146. The severity of the climb can be gauged by the relationship of the viaduct parapet to the horizon! *(Photo: R. E. Toop. Date: 12 June 1965.)*

When this area was first revisited, the viaduct could not be seen and was completely overgrown by a mass of elder. 'Keeping Bath Tidy' entered my mind, so I attempted a little pruning before taking this shot. Mike Arlett risked his bad back by joining me on the climb up the slope to the vantage point from which I took this photo! However despite my concern for him, it was I that went base over apex on the descent! Photographs of this area are fairly rare due to it being difficult to locate. This was much to the chagrin of photographer Derek Cross who could never find Lyncombe Vale. Note the subtle change to the scene on the horizon. *(Date: 5 July 1985.)*

13
Combe Down Tunnel
(172 ST 755 632)

The 'Down' 'Pines Express' hauled by Class '2P' 4-4-0 No 40563 and Stanier 'Black Five' 4-6-0 No 44839, over the small viaduct near the northern entrance of Combe Down Tunnel. It is hard to believe this beautiful wooded scene was so close to the city centre about one mile away. *(Photo: Ivo Peters. Date: May 1953.)*

The only visible reminders seen in this photograph of trees are the viaduct railings near the centre of the picture, which was taken from the top of Combe Down Tunnel's northern parapet. Walking back down Lyncombe Vale, I startled a fox who jumped down onto the old track-bed in front of me, decided that he disliked me intensely and shot back up the slope from whence he came!

Combe Down Tunnel now belongs to the Wessex Water Authority. Its portals have been fitted with massive steel doors faced with concrete so entry by the public is impossible. *(Date: 14 June 1985.)*

14
Horsecombe Vale
(172 ST 763 618)

BR Class '5' No 73052 and Stanier 'Black Five' No 45440 charge up the 1:55 gradient towards Combe Down Tunnel through the beautiful Horsecombe Vale with the 14.45 (SO) Bournemouth to Bristol on a glorious high summer's afternoon with eight on! No 73052 was coupled up front to save a light engine path having to be found. Note Tucking Mill Viaduct in the background. *(Photo: Ivo Peters. Date: 2 July 1955.)*

Mother Nature has taken over this spot now, although the track-bed remains reasonably clear. Near this location the remains of the lineside telephone box at the southern end of Combe Down Tunnel can still be seen. The growth of trees has obscured the view to Tucking Mill Viaduct which still stands. The viaduct provides a majestic backdrop to Tucking Mill Pond which now has fishing facilities for disabled persons. *(Date: 14 June 1985.)*

15
Near Midford Castle
(172 ST 762 611)

With the continuing demise of the S&D '7F's, Stanier '8F's began to appear on the Somerset & Dorset. Stanier Class '8F' 2-8-0 No 48737 takes the 08.15 'Down' local from Bath to Templecombe past the grounds of Midford Castle, coasting towards Midford Station. Due to lack of steam heating on all but two of the class (only one thus equipped was allocated to the S&D), they could not be used on passenger trains after the end of September. Note the white horse in the field. *(Photo: Ivo Peters. Date: 28 September 1963.)*

The trees on the horizon provide a link with the previous photograph since the track side has overgrown. The odd concrete post can still be identified as being the same as on the original. Ivo Peters asked me why I could not have arranged for a white horse to appear in this photo and why I could only manage a chestnut mare! The answer was simple—I left my cans of aerosol paint behind—sorry Ivo! *(Date: 24 June 1985.)*

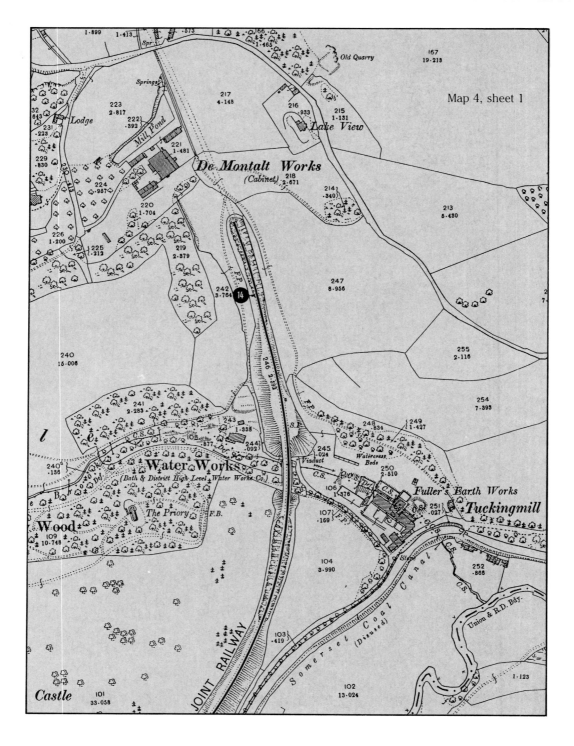

Map 4, 1904/1930: Horse-combe Vale/Tucking Mill to Midford

Sheet 1 (1904)

This map shows the south portal of Combe Down Tunnel, from which the line emerged into Horsecombe Vale and crossed over Tucking Mill Viaduct, this latter having been widened to accept double track.

The land just to the north of the viaduct was also widened by the railway company between 1892/4 for doubling of the line to Bath and in anticipation of a station being built to serve Combe Down. In the event the double track ended on Midford Viaduct and the plans to construct the station or halt were never realized. Note the waterworks and the Fullers Earth works, also the defunct Somersetshire Coal Canal which are all shown to advantage on this interesting map.

Sheet 2 (1904)

The line meanders southwards passing the grounds of Midford Castle (quaintly built to form the shape of the Ace of Clubs, set high upon a hill) and the small goods yard from which Fullers Earth sent up from Tucking Mill Works was transported. The yard is situated just to the north of a 66-yard tunnel known as 'The Long Arch Bridge' passing under Tucking Mill Lane.

The disused Camerton arm of the Somersetshire Coal Canal can be seen running parallel to the railway until passing at almost 90° underneath the eight-arch Midford Viaduct. After its completion in 1910 the GWR Camerton to Limpley Stoke branch line also passed under the S&D over another viaduct of its own (see 1930 map). The Hope and Anchor Inn is sandwiched between the old canal bed and the station located on the 'Up' side of the line, above it.

The point at which the S&D track became double, altered in the line's history, being nearer the northern end of the viaduct in 1902: in 1933 it was moved nearer the southern end.

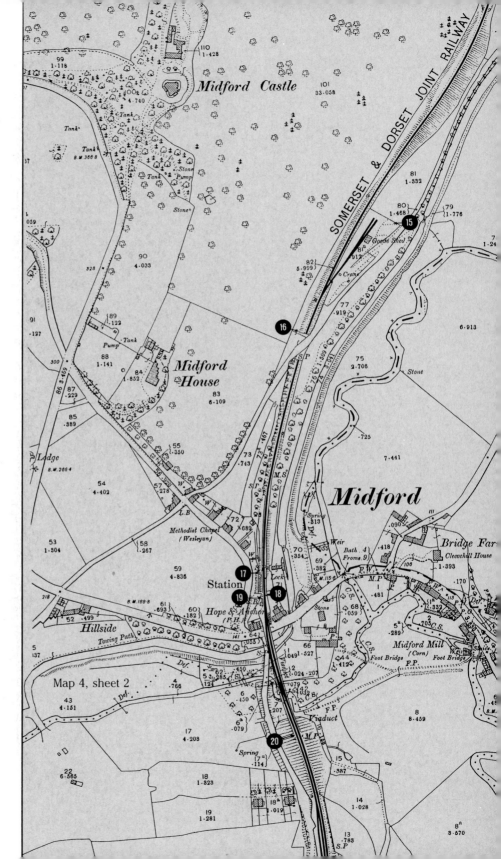

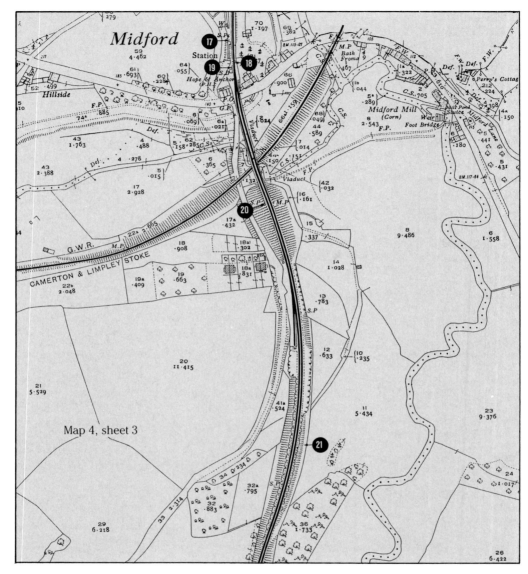

Map 4, sheet 3

The short siding on the 'Up' side is seen at the south side of the Viaduct. The course of the old Somersetshire Coal Canal's tramway from Radstock had once crossed diagonally near to the position of the siding's points. The small parcels of land adjacent to the railway on the right provide the clue to this.

Midford Station platform survives today and is the subject of a preser-vation attempt by a group of enthus-iasts. The site of the signal box, a flat-roofed affair rebuilt as such after a contretemps with some wagons shed from a runaway train in 1936, is now part of the car park for the Hope and Anchor.

Sheet 3 (1930)

This map shows the GWR Camer-ton to Limpley Stoke branch line, completed in 1910, passing under the S&D.

The branch closed to passenger traffic in 1925, having been sus-pended during World War I. It remained in use for mineral traffic from the Camerton Collieries until final closure in 1951. During the summer of 1952, the line was used to make the Ealing Studio's classic comedy 'The Titfield Thunderbolt'; Monkton Combe Station being re-named 'Titfield'. The track was lifted in 1958.

16
Midford Station goods yard
(172 ST 761 611)

S&D '7F' No 53809 trundles past
Midford's goods yard with the 15.48
goods from Bath, known to S&D
folk as 'The Market'; it served all
stations between Radstock and
Evercreech. Note the small goods
shed and crane (replaced circa
1952) in the yard from where Fullers
Earth was once transported. The
ground frame (Midford 'A') controlled the entrance to the goods
yard. This photo was taken from
'The Long Arch Bridge'. *(Photo: Ivo
Peters. Date: 21 April 1951.)*

Today the scene is plain to see. The
track-bed leading under the short
37-yard tunnel, 'The Long Arch
Bridge', is used for 'doggie walking'
from the station at Midford to Tucking Mill Viaduct. The view of the
trees in the background remains
largely unchanged. This photo was
notoriously difficult to obtain due to
bad lighting and a surfeit of elder
saplings, and had to be taken before
the trees sprouted foliage! *(Date: 10
April 1985.)*

17
Midford Station (1)
(172 ST 761 607)

'2P' 4-4-0 No 40697 drifting over Midford Viaduct on an 'Up' local is about to catch the tablet for the single line working to Bath Junction. Note the tablet arm extended in readiness; the footplate crew of the '2P' peer over the side of the cab to see that all goes well. The flat roof of the signal box was the result of rebuilding after an uninvited meeting with some trucks shed from a runaway train in 1936. Note also the roof of the station building and the skylight at the end under which was the gents' loo! The old track of the GWR Camerton-Limpley Stoke branch can be seen passing underneath the viaduct. The roof of the 'Hope and Anchor' inn is that on the left of the picture. The photograph was taken from the tall backing signal on the station platform. *(Photo: Ivo Peters. Date: 1955.)*

A photograph taken from the same spot shows the remains of Midford's platform and the tiled floor of the lavatory! The viaduct can be seen through the trees. The two houses on the far side provide a good reference point to the 1955 photograph. The car park in the foreground is now that of the 'Hope and Anchor' inn. The foundations of the old signal box can still be discerned on its surface. *(Date: 14 June 1985.)*

18
Midford Station (2) (172 ST 761 607)

S&D '7F' No 53805 passes Midford Station with a train of coal empties for Radstock. Note the porters' cabin in front of the tall backing signal. The lamp room can just be seen behind the coal trucks towards the middle of the picture. Also of interest, is how the station was built on a steep embankment, having been hewn out of the hillside. This photo was taken from the 'Down' starting signal. *(Photo: The late Derek Cross, via D. M. Cross. Date: July 1960.)*

There are some shots that need to be taken from an elevated position, as in this case, from the site of Midford's 'Down' starting signal. I have devised a rather 'Heath Robinson' piece of equipment upon which a camera is mounted in order to effect such a shot. When Mike Arlett first saw this apparatus being erected in the Hope and Anchor's car park, bringing looks of astonishment from the patrons, he almost refused to be associated with me! 'Is this where I leave?' he asked. However, a 'pint' bet was made as to my success or not—a pint that I was subsequently to enjoy with great relish!

The station is the subject of a restoration attempt, the artefacts of such can be seen stacked on the platform which has been cleared of undergrowth. Since this photograph was taken some rails of light gauge have been laid at the northern end to form a tramway some 30 yards in length, along which trucks are hauled by a hand-operated vehicle. *(Date: 14 June 1985.)*

19
Midford Station (3)
(172 ST 761 607)

Ivatt 2-6-2T No 41243 brings the 18.05 Bath to Binegar local to a stand at Midford's platform. A good impression can be obtained of the curved nature of the platform. The lamp room is seen clearly in the background, viewed from the signal box steps. *(Photo: The late Derek Cross via D. M. Cross. Date: 11 August 1961.)*

The platform has been cleared awaiting restoration but the base of the lavatory can be seen on the left. Note also the retaining wall previously hidden behind the station buildings. *(Date: 14 June 1985.)*

20
Midford Viaduct
(172 ST 761 605)

Class '4F' 0-6-0 No 44417 on the 15.20 Bath to Templecombe local takes the 'Down' line onto the double track section which was gained on Midford Viaduct. The track and viaduct for the GWR Camerton-Limpley Stoke branch can be seen passing underneath. The 'Hope and Anchor' inn is visible above the engine.

Signalman Percy Savage's cottage is seen nestling up to the viaduct on the left, in front of which an arm of the Somersetshire Coal Canal ran, as does Cam Brook. This fine study of Midford was taken from the 'Up' inner home signal. *(Photo: Ivo Peters. Date: 7 June 1958.)*

The viaduct remains intact and although the railings have lost much of their white paint it still manages to look dignified in its retirement. The track-bed remains in good condition, if a little overgrown with weed. Surprisingly little seems to have changed, except for the odd new house and trees having grown; notice Midford Castle on the horizon which was obscured by trees in the original photograph. The track-bed of the old GWR Camerton branch is now hidden, although by peering over the viaduct it can still be seen clearly. *(Date: 14 June 1985.)*

21
Midford Valley
(172 ST 762 602)

'2P' No 40652 pilots rebuilt Bulleid Pacific 4-6-2 No 34039, *Boscastle*, on the 'Up' 'Pines Express' through the reverse curves just south of Midford Viaduct. The Midford 'Up' outer home signal can be seen above the first coach. 'Up' trains often had to wait here for the single line section from Bath Junction to Midford to clear before proceeding on their journey. A lineside telephone was sited near the signal post in a small concrete hut to enable train crews to telephone Midford box to enquire as to the delay, if they were held up for a time. Engine crews were often threatened with a longer wait if the vernacular was used to express their concern to the signalman at any delay caused by the single line section already being occupied! *(Photo: Ivo Peters. Date: 20 June 1959.)*

The track-bed is well defined in this section and is kept tidy by cattle that are frequently allowed to graze here. The base of the 'Up' outer home signal, together with the remains of the lineside hut, are still to be seen in the undergrowth. Various shrubs and bushes can still be identified as those that appear in the 1959 photograph—but it takes a keen eye to spot them! *(Date: 8 June 1985.)*

22
Midford Valley—Lower Twinhoe (172 ST 756 592)

Standard Class '4' 4-6-0 No 75023 which was a Templecombe engine and recently acquired, pilots Standard Class '5' 4-6-0 No 73047 with the 'Down' 'Pines Express' through the lovely Midford Valley, near Lower Twinhoe. The line was engineered to follow the old Somersetshire Coal Canal and Tramway as closely as possible, hence the severe curvature of the line formation. The Midford 'Up' distant signal can be seen to the left of the train, half-way round the bend.

It was adjacent to this point at Lower Twinhoe that the Radstock arm of the Somersetshire Coal Canal ended, to continue on from here to Midford as a tramway. This was due to lack of finance to complete the system, linking it with the Camerton Arm, requiring a large flight of locks to be built to take it to a lower level at Midford. *(Photo: G. A. Richardson, via Peter Smith. Date: September 1961.)*

The line formation is now used as a farm track and remains in reasonable condition, although some brambles had to be cut before this shot could be effected. The lineside is abundant with blackthorn and other varieties of scrub—as well as an ample dung heap!

A further expedition to this area revealed the actual formation of the old coal canal set against the hillside immediately to the left of this photograph, some 10 or 15ft above the level of the S&D's track-bed. Note the similarities on the horizon. *(Date: 8 June 1985.)*

23
Midford Valley
(172 ST 755 592)

Class '2P' No 40700, looking as if it has received some treatment to its front end, comes around the bend from Lower Twinhoe towards Wellow with a 'Down' stopping train from Bath.

The Somersetshire Coal Canal had also passed through this cutting near Hankley Wood, albeit at a higher level, before terminating further round the bend towards Lower Twinhoe. When the railway

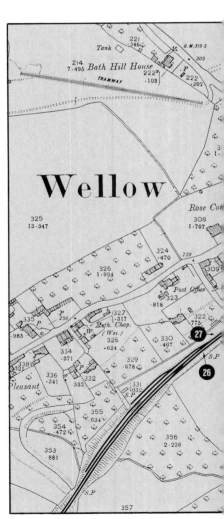

was constructed, the cutting was deepened and the line was then built on a rising gradient (which was 1:100 at this point) towards Wellow. *(Photo: Ivo Peters. Date: 11 May 1957.)*

The beautiful countryside in the Midford Valley remains largely unaffected by the passage of time. The course of Wellow Brook can be seen, meandering through the valley below. The horizon has sprouted a water tower. Fortunately it is not too obtrusive being surrounded by mature trees. *(Date: 8 June 1985.)*

Chapter 3
Wellow—
Radstock

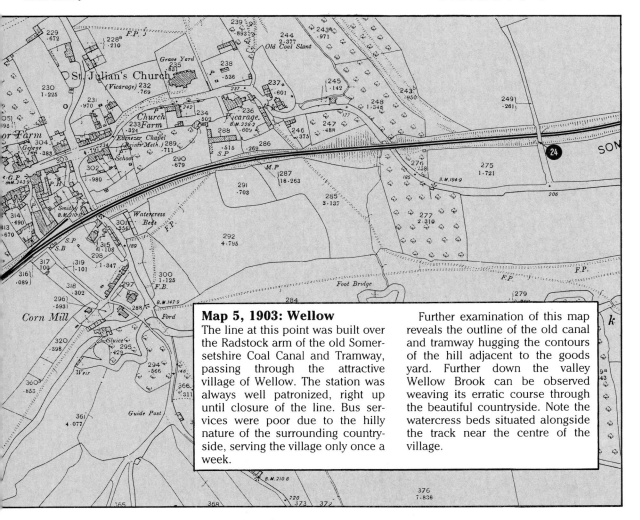

Map 5, 1903: Wellow
The line at this point was built over the Radstock arm of the old Somersetshire Coal Canal and Tramway, passing through the attractive village of Wellow. The station was always well patronized, right up until closure of the line. Bus services were poor due to the hilly nature of the surrounding countryside, serving the village only once a week.

Further examination of this map reveals the outline of the old canal and tramway hugging the contours of the hill adjacent to the goods yard. Further down the valley Wellow Brook can be observed weaving its erratic course through the beautiful countryside. Note the watercress beds situated alongside the track near the centre of the village.

24
Wellow (172 ST 746 583)

On a cloudless summer's day the 'Up' 'Pines Express' passes over Wellow Viaduct in the mid distance, hauled by '2P' No 40564 and rebuilt S.R. Pacific No 34046, *Braunton*. The fourteenth century St Julian's Church can be seen dominating this small village, which is surrounded by hills. This photograph was taken from a farm bridge just off the Hinton Charterhouse road nearby. *(Photo: Ivo Peters. Date: 18 June 1960.)*

Again taken on a perfect early summer's day, the church tower still commands the view. The line formation has become a farm track, adjacent to which can be seen the end of a piggery's yard. Notice the abundance of early summer's blossom on the bushes covering the embankments. *(Date: 8 June 1985.)*

25
Wellow Station (1)
(172 ST 739 581)

S&D '7F' No 53807 reverses into the goods yard at Wellow to allow the 'Up' 'Pines Express' through. The driver looks behind to make sure that all is well, whilst the fireman leaning out of the cab seems to be lost in his thoughts!

A good view of the well patronized Wellow Station and its buildings on the 'Up' platform is offered by this fine study. The church tower can be seen behind the chimney to the right of the picture. *(Photo: R. C. Riley. Date: 6 July 1959.)*

Tussocks of grass cover this section of line. The goods yard is now used as a car park. The station is a private dwelling and is in fine condition. Note how the trees have grown up on the left since 1959. *(Date: 25 June 1985.)*

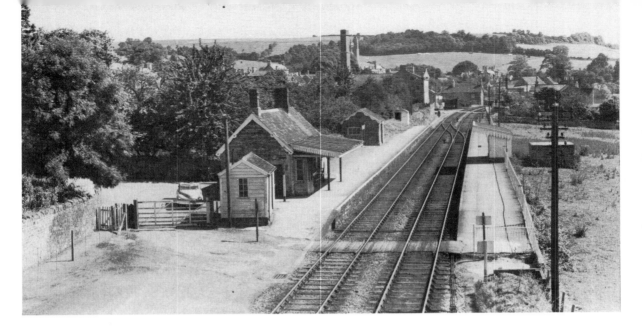

26
Wellow Station (2)
(172 ST 739 581)

A view of Wellow Station and village taken from the 'Down' starting signal. The layout of the platforms and buildings can be seen to good advantage. Note the photographer's car behind the goods yard gate! (It would be worth a small fortune today!) *(Photo: R. C. Riley. Date: 6 July 1959.)*

A similar evening study taken 26 years later reveals the obvious changes. The well-kept grass of the old station house provides its owners with a croquet lawn. Note the 'Down' platform adorned with flower tubs, upon which the owner intends to rebuild the small shelter seen in the original photograph, which will make a nice summer house. The old goods yard gate can be seen in the undergrowth in the immediate foreground. *(Date: 5 July 1985.)*

27
Wellow Station (3)
(172 ST 739 581)

The ubiquitous 18.05 (SX) Bath to Binegar local hauled by 'Jinty' '3F' No 47465 blowing off steam impatiently, waits to get under way again from Wellow with its train.

The neat and tidy appearance of this S&D designed station can be gauged from the photograph. The goods yard gate can just be seen on the left of the picture. *(Photo: Ivo Peters. Date: 12 April 1954.)*

A garden fence has been erected across the platform ramps where the railings are still clearly visible on the 'Down' side. The station sign has been preserved and is well cared for. Note the goods yard gate in the foreground.

Insert The last signal box left on the line once housed an eighteen-lever frame. The box is now owned by the artist Peter Blake. *(Date: 2 May 1985.)*

28
Wellow Valley
(172 ST 733 576)

Through the lovely Wellow Valley
south-west of the village, the line
continued to follow as closely as
possible the route of the old tramway laid along the towpath of the
old Somersetshire Coal Canal. Its
remnants can be seen on the right
of this photograph showing BR
Class '5' 4-6-0 No 73050 with the
16.45 'Up' freight from Evercreech
Junction enjoying the evening sunshine. *(Photo: Ivo Peters. Date: 8
July 1958.)*

Evening shadows steal across the
beautiful landscape of Wellow
Valley. The line in the foreground
has been obscured by trees and
bushes. A large poultry unit has
been built on the section where the
canal and tramway could once be
seen. Its roof is just visible now
through the trees. The location is a
haven for rabbits that scattered
every which way upon my appearance on the scene! (One cannot
blame them!) Note the old line
formation in the middle distance.
(Date: 25 June 1985.)

29
Shoscombe and Single Hill Halt (172 ST 719 561)

'If there's anyone for here—this is it!' called out a guard of an 'Up' local one dark night as it drew into the halt!

The station was a latecomer and was not opened until 23 September 1929. The platforms were built of concrete and were sparse—no buildings or shelters provided. One particular local man used to walk back along the line from Radstock after a night out in the town, (playing in a local silver band), which saved considerable puff by not having to climb up and down the steep hills that surround the village —it also reduced the risk of getting lost if he had over-imbibed, but not, perhaps, the risk of being squashed by a train! *(Photo: courtesy Mrs Anne Scott. Date: 20 June 1959.)*

The station has been completely demolished and the site forms two or three small paddocks in one of which can be seen children's paraphernalia. The only reference to the station is provided by two concrete posts in the middle of the picture which mark the top of a flight of steps which led from the road below to the 'Down' platform. These can be seen at the end of the platform ramp in the 1959 picture. *(Date: 2 May 1985.)*

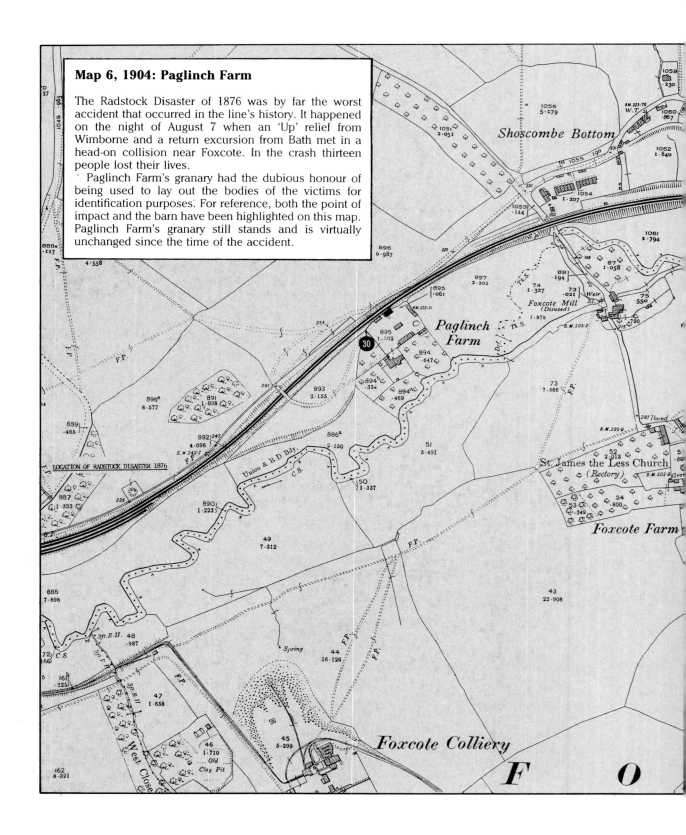

Map 6, 1904: Paglinch Farm

The Radstock Disaster of 1876 was by far the worst accident that occurred in the line's history. It happened on the night of August 7 when an 'Up' relief from Wimborne and a return excursion from Bath met in a head-on collision near Foxcote. In the crash thirteen people lost their lives.

· Paglinch Farm's granary had the dubious honour of being used to lay out the bodies of the victims for identification purposes. For reference, both the point of impact and the barn have been highlighted on this map. Paglinch Farm's granary still stands and is virtually unchanged since the time of the accident.

Shoscombe Bottom

Foxcote Mill
(Disused)

Paglinch
Farm

St. James the Less Church
(Rectory)

Foxcote Farm

LOCATION OF RADSTOCK DISASTER 1876

Union & R.D. Bdy.

Spring

Old
Clay Pit

West Close

Foxcote Colliery

F O

30
Paglinch Farm
(172 ST 711 557)

S&D '7F' No 53809 passes the granary of Paglinch Farm with a southbound goods. This was the barn in which the bodies of the thirteen unfortunate victims of the 1876 Radstock Disaster were laid out for identification. This sad tale had an unfortunate twist to it, for the return excursion from Bath, in which the people were killed, was chosen in preference to their returning to Radstock via the GWR line from Bristol, which they had been visiting that day. *(Photo: R. E. Toop. Date: 27 December 1961.)*

Today the barn is unchanged and has probably remained so since it was built. Note that the yard gate seen in the original photograph is now propped up against the wall. The line of railway fence posts can still be seen in the foreground. The wooden posts carry an electric fence to restrain our bovine friends and are actually positioned on the line of the 'Down' track's near side rail and apparently were the very devil to drive-in!

It took three visits here to effect a satisfactory shot, mostly due to adverse weather conditions. On the first occasion my car sump received severe punishment on a farm track; on the second visit the car was up to its hub caps in liquified bovine fertilizer—ah well, the things one does to please one's public! *(Date: 2 May 1985.)*

Map 7, 1904: Lower Writhlington

The S&D entered the Somerset coal fields at Writhlington. Sidings were built on the south and east sides to
serve the collieries at Writhlington and to the north side
to serve the colliery at Braysdown, which had a 2ft 6in
gauge incline plane to the pit head set on the hill above.

    The Writhlington Collieries' tramway was 2ft 8½in
gauge, one section of which can be seen leading to the
Upper Writhlington Colliery. Today, some dozen or more
years after the closure of Writhlington, coal is still being
extracted from the adjacent tip.

31
Lower Writhlington Colliery
(172 ST 706 555)

BR '9F' 2-10-0 No 92000, the doyen
of the class built at Crewe in 1953,
passes Writhlington Colliery with a
Bournemouth to Bristol train. Seeing large engines rostered on such a
light duty some two years later did
not help the cost-effectiveness of
the S&D.

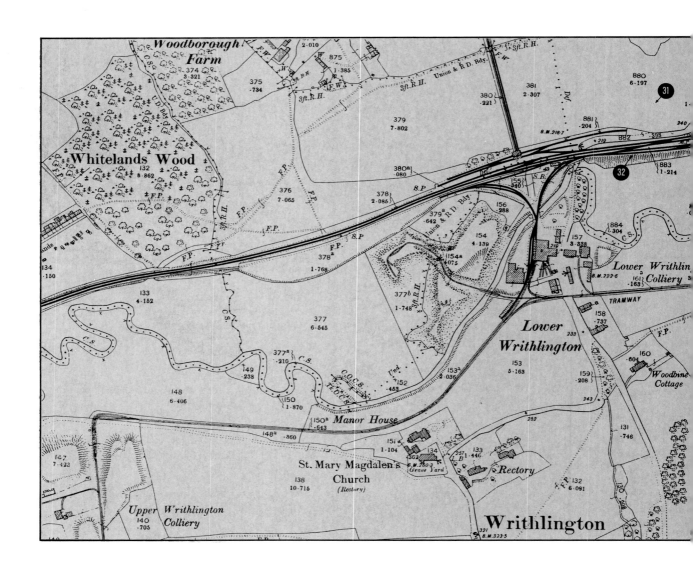

Note the pithead winding wheels and screens of Writhlington Colliery, together with trucks being loaded with coal. The signal box controlled the colliery sidings. The remains of Braysdown Colliery sidings can be seen to the right of the bridge. An incline plane from the pit at the top of the hill was used to take coal down to the screens below. *(Photo: The late Derek Cross, via D. M. Cross. Date: 15 August 1961.)*

Writhlington Colliery was finally closed in 1973, but coal extraction is still taking place today—some twelve or thirteen per cent of it being recovered from the tip in the background. Heavy plant can be seen crawling like ants over the summit. Notice how the tip has changed since 1961—there being a further twelve years of mining before closure.

The North Derbyshire firm of Burrows, who specialize in coal extraction, are using the Barnaby Dense Medium Washer System in the recovery of reasonable quality coking coal from the tip. When the work is complete the slag heap will be landscaped and planted with 25,000 indigenous trees using the hydro process.

The water bowser seen on the right is used to keep down coal dust on the line formation to Radstock which is being utilized by heavy lorries carrying coal from the tip. Work is to last another year or more and is carried on by twelve-hour shifts, seven days a week. The photographs were taken from the top of a pillbox.

Wellow Brook can be seen in both photographs on the left. Today there are only one or two original buildings left on the colliery site, the rest were demolished a few years ago. *(Date: 10 April 1985.)*

32
Writhlington Colliery
Sidings (172 ST 706 554)

'Jinty' 0-6-0T No 47316 busily collecting a few trucks from Writhlington Sidings, which can be seen to be fairly extensive. The cow on the left is actually on the road leading up to Peasedown St John from Writhlington! Just a few hundred yards around the bend behind the engine, was the site of the 1876 accident near Foxcote. *(Photo: R. E. Toop. Date: 27 December 1961.)*

It is ironic that the last section of S&D track to remain was between Radstock and Writhlington sidings, lingering on till late 1975 and into the early months of 1976, when it was finally lifted. This accounts for the reasonable state of the track bed still apparent here. The solitary telegraph pole on the right provides the link with yesteryear. *(Date: 2 May 1985.)*

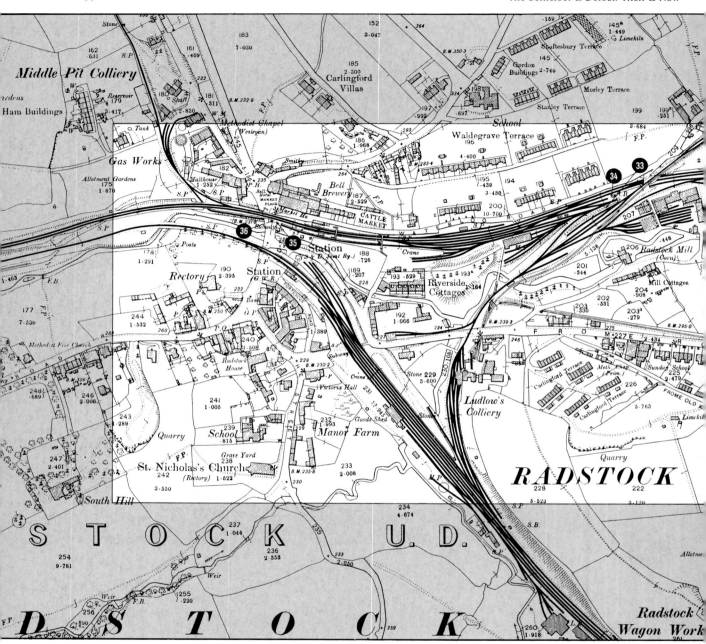

Map 8, 1904: Radstock

Radstock was the centre for the Somerset mining industry, now but a memory. Middle Pit, Tyning Colliery and Ludlow's Colliery can clearly be seen together with their network of tramways. The map shows how the railways could dominate a small town. Radstock was served by two stations, Radstock North (S&D) and Radstock West (GWR) which were only a matter of yards apart!

The map of 1904 indicates that all the tramways in this area were by this date converted to the standard 4ft 8½in gauge, the one exception being the tramway serving Ludlow's and Tyning Colliery which was of 3ft 2in gauge, being converted to 2ft gauge about 1909 after Tyning pit's closure. Thereafter the standard gauge connection to Tyning Colliery over the famous low-arched Tyning Bridge (affectionately known as

'Marble Arch') became redundant.

The map also shows that a section of the standard gauge tramway between 'Marble Arch' and Tyning pit had a common centre rail and a passing loop, possibly because of limited space available when shared with the narrow gauge tramway. 'Marble Arch', which had a clearance of approximately 10ft 10in, can be seen just to the north of the wagon works, diagonally crossing the S&D line.

Map 9, 1982: Radstock

Radstock has not severed its railway links completely. Extensive sidings on the former GWR Bristol to Frome line goods yard south of the town are still used by the Marcroft Wagon Repair Works. Today sheltered housing has been built on the former Radstock S&D goods yard— the station now completely demolished and the area landscaped.

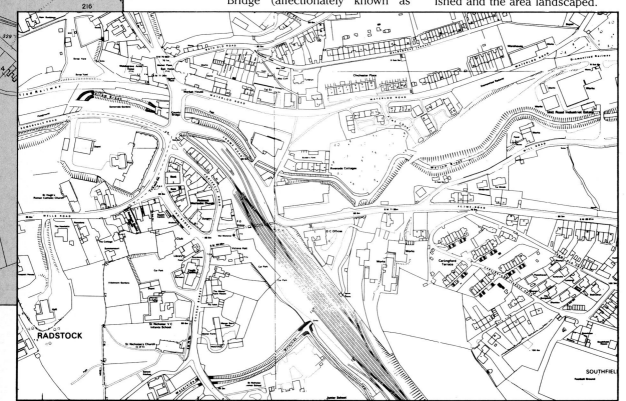

33
Tyning Bridge—'Marble Arch', Radstock
(172/183 ST 693 550)

One of three Highbridge-built 0-4-0 STs, No 26a emerges from the 10ft 10in clearance of 'Marble Arch'. Only the smallest of engines were capable of working the sidings the other side of the bridge. This fine photograph was taken in the same year as these diminutive locomotives were withdrawn and replaced by two Sentinel 0-4-0s of unorthodox design. No 26a is looking far removed from the condition that the nickname of *Dazzler* would suggest, as she and her two sisters were affectionately known.

The arch was almost certainly that built over the Somersetshire Coal Canal tramway to connect Tyning Pit and Ludlow Colliery and eventually the GWR yard.

Radstock (North) 'A' signal box can be seen on the left of the photograph. It was a tall structure, facilitating a view over and beyond Tyning Bridge and the east. 'A' Box controlled the goods yard and the approach to the two road engine shed. This was still called 'Radstock East Box' in 1929, but was re-named Radstock (North) 'A' after nationalisation. *(Photo: H. C. Casserley. Date: 16 March 1929.)*

The 'new' Tyning Bridge and 'Marble Arch' have gone—only parapets remain, but note the steps visible on the left that were from the Radstock (North) 'A' Box. Careful study of the photograph will reveal that a rail section post at the top right, appears in both photographs. Tyning Pit was further up the hill shown top centre, whilst the main S&D line ran diagonally in front of the parapet in the background. *(Date: 14 June 1985.)*

34
Radstock goods yard and shed (172/183 ST 693 550)

BR Standard Class '5' 4-6-0 No 73049 heads towards Bath with a three-coach train past Radstock (North) 'A' signal box. The stone-built engine shed is on the left of the picture. A famous Radstock landmark in the form of the Co-op building is in the background: next to it can be seen one of the station's footbridges. Note the stone-built terraced cottages which are indigenous to this area. *(Photo: The late Derek Cross via D. M. Cross. Date: 8 June 1964.)*

The remains of the track-bed in the foreground is littered with debris slung over the wall. The new sheltered housing development built on the site of the goods yard and engine shed is appropriately called 'Pine Court'! The cottages remain unaffected by the passage of time. This photograph was taken from the site of the old Radstock (North) 'A' signal box adjacent to the remains of 'Marble Arch'. *(Date: 14 June 1985.)*

35
Radstock (North) Station
(172/183 ST 689 550)

A view looking in the 'Up' direction through the station. In the foreground is the wall of the subway (Bridge No 40). The 'Up' platform housed the main station buildings, whilst the 'Down' side had only a shelter but the station boasted two footbridges, the second of which can be seen in the background and provided access from the adjacent Waterloo Road. The building in the same complex as the Market and ex-Oak Hill Brewery on the left with the round windows and just seen behind the station is a public lavatory!

Note the gradient post under the station sign indicating the start of the climb south towards Masbury at 1:55. Just a few yards south of here was the GWR station, whose line ran parallel to the S&D's across the A367 road. *(Photo: Lens of Sutton. Date: 1960.)*

The area has been totally landscaped in the foreground, and beyond a shoppers' car park has been provided. In the distance can be seen 'Pine Court' sheltered housing, built on the site of the goods yard and engine shed. The public convenience has closed, whilst the building on the left has not changed to any great degree. The station buildings were demolished in the late '70s and the subway filled in. *(Date: 30 May 1985.)*

36
Radstock Crossing—A367
(172/183 ST 689 550)

Everything has to stop for the passage of S&D '7F' No 53805 on an 'Up' Evercreech Junction to Bath goods over the busy A367 road. This crossing caused (and still causes) considerable traffic congestion, especially since the GWR Bristol-Frome line crossed within yards south of this point.

Of interest in this photograph, behind the railings in the foreground, is the track path of the tramway which ran under the main line to Middle Pit Colliery. The site also marked the basin of the Somersetshire Coal Canal.

This photograph was taken from the steps of Radstock (North) 'B' signal box. *(Photo: The late Derek Cross, via D. M. Cross. Date: June 1960.)*

The emptiness of the road is deceptive to say the least! I was perched on top of a tall pair of steps to obtain this study, taken during a lull in the traffic. The photograph shows clearly the course of the S&D which is now the start of a Linear Park sponsored by Wansdyke District Council, the path leading up the old line towards the 'Five Arches Bridge' a few hundred yards away. (Note the old railings still apparent.)

Beyond 'Five Arches' the bridge over Somervale Road was demolished in 1982. The park is to extend beyond this point and the Norton Hill Colliery slag heap, which is still owned by the NCB, will be developed into a leisure area, including a car park (near the spur to the GWR), a café and a hill-fort for children. The whole area will be landscaped, including extensive tree planting. The council will not proceed, however, until assurances are given by the NCB as to the stability of the slag heap. *(Date: 30 May 1985.)*

Chapter 4
Midsomer Norton—Binegar

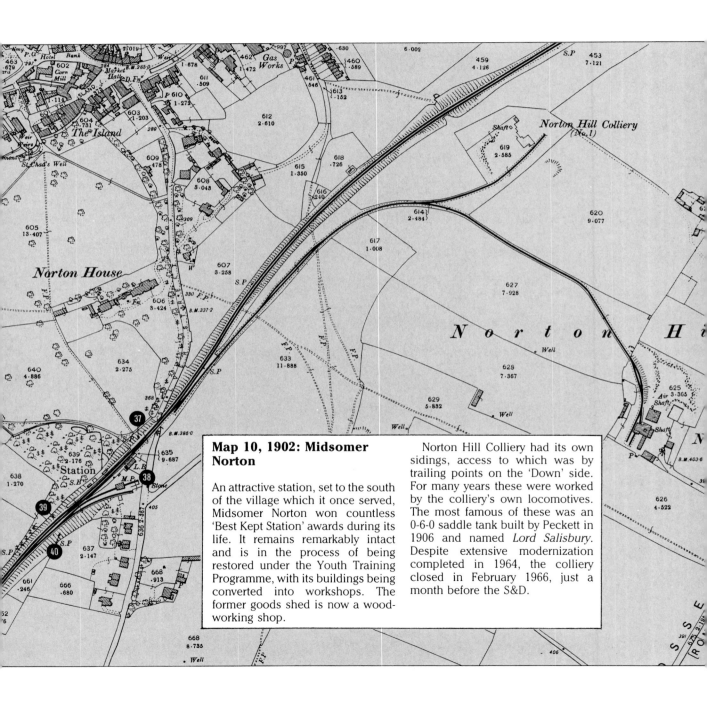

Map 10, 1902: Midsomer Norton

An attractive station, set to the south of the village which it once served, Midsomer Norton won countless 'Best Kept Station' awards during its life. It remains remarkably intact and is in the process of being restored under the Youth Training Programme, with its buildings being converted into workshops. The former goods shed is now a wood-working shop.

Norton Hill Colliery had its own sidings, access to which was by trailing points on the 'Down' side. For many years these were worked by the colliery's own locomotives. The most famous of these was an 0-6-0 saddle tank built by Peckett in 1906 and named *Lord Salisbury*. Despite extensive modernization completed in 1964, the colliery closed in February 1966, just a month before the S&D.

37
Midsomer Norton (Bridge No 48) (183 ST 664 537)

47 years separates the date that these engines were built! 'Auntie' '3F' 0-6-0 No 43216 of 1902 vintage pilots SR Pacific No 34093 *Saunton* across the bridge (under which the B3355 passes) and towards Midsomer Norton Station. Midsomer Norton's 'Down' home signal seen over the train stood in the 'V' formed between the main line and the sidings of Norton Hill Colliery in the background. *(Photo: Ivo Peters. Date: 1 August 1953.)*

The bridge has been demolished—the area landscaped—the steep line formation of the S&D is just visible to the left of the street lamp, just to the right of which can be seen the old track of Norton Hill Colliery's sidings. The old tree on the right provides continuity—albeit a little thin on top now! *(Date: 29 May 1985.)*

38
Midsomer Norton Station (1)
(183 ST 664 537)

S&D '7F' No 53806 2-8-0 has picked up a short coal train from Norton Hill Colliery and is about to proceed to Bath.

Some of the lovely flowers of Midsomer Norton Station can be seen adorning the shelter on the 'Up' platform. Ivo Peters relates that one year it did not win the annual competition held as to which was the best kept—after a long run of winning—causing astonishment to all and sundry. One person expressing his surprise as to the outcome learned the possible reason when he was asked, 'Ah yes, but didn't you see the copper pipework in the toilets?' which really summed up the pride S&D men had in the appearance of their stations. Midsomer Norton also seemed to have more than its fair share of handcarts, judging from this photograph! *(Photo: The late Derek Cross, via D. M. Cross. Date: July 1960.)*

Sometime after closure and as part of a project for the nearby Somervale School, the platforms were filled in, but today they are again visible and now the site is receiving attention from a YTS Project. The shelter on the 'Up' platform is being re-clad and painted. The railings on the 'Up' side have received a new coat of white paint since this photo was taken. Thankfully the station appears to have a bright future! *(Date: 14 June 1985.)*

39
Midsomer Norton Station (2)
(183 ST 664 536)

The twelve-coach train of the 10.38 (SO) Manchester to Bournemouth is brought up through Midsomer Norton Station by a pair of '4F' 0-6-0s, Nos 44557 and 44559, struggling to haul their heavy load up the 1:50 gradient to the station.

The attractive sixteen-lever signal box provides a good vantage point for the signalman to give the train crews a cheery wave as they pass by. The stone goods shed can also be seen to good advantage in this photograph. *(Photo: Ivo Peters. Date: 6 August 1955.)*

The late afternoon sun shines on the station buildings on a glorious spring day showing them to good advantage. The nearest chimney on the station building was replaced at a cost of £1,500. The goods shed has been turned into a woodworking shop for the YTS. The flat roofed building on the right is used by the County of Avon Parks and Gardens Department as a store. *(Date: 29 May 1985.)*

40
Midsomer Norton Station (3)
(183 ST 664 536)

BR Class '4' 2-6-0 No 76015 and BR Class '5' 4-6-0 No 73050 pass through Midsomer Norton Station with a Whit Monday excursion to Bournemouth from Bristol. This was still a popular way for the public to enjoy a day out. A panoramic view of the station layout is seen to good advantage. In the background are Norton Hill Colliery sidings with coal trucks in residence. *(Photo: Ivo Peters. Date: 5 June 1960.)*

Two visits had to be made to this site to clear undergrowth and prune overhanging branches in order to obtain this photograph. This was achieved by propping up a pair of steps with a plank of wood against a steep bank, having fallen off the steps during a dummy run in the process! Due to the growth of saplings and trees, it was impossible to get into the precise position from which the original photograph was taken.

Insert To the rear of the spot where I was perched, the old loading gauge could still be seen peering out over the top of a spoil heap built around it! *(29 May 1985.)*

41
Chilcompton Tunnel Cutting
(183 ST 652 523)

Recently back from overhaul at Derby, '2P' No 40568 pilots 'West Country' Pacific No 34093 *Saunton* climbing up the 1:53 gradient through the deep-sided cutting towards Chilcompton Tunnel on the 'Down' 'Pines' relief. Midsomer Norton lay around the curve seen in the far distance.

This was one of Ivo Peters' favourite locations and certainly provided a fine vantage point from which to photograph steam. *(Photo: Ivo Peters. Date: 16 June 1951.)*

Oh dear! Thousands of tons of backfilling have returned the land back to a meadow which it was 100 years or so before, making the location very difficult to pinpoint! Just a fraction of the line formation can be seen, sweeping round the curve back towards Midsomer Norton in the distance.

Just out of sight in the foreground there was a large bull attending his cows, so while he was fully engaged I took advantage to sit on the grass awaiting the sun to reappear from behind slow-moving clouds! Various trees can be identified as the same as those appearing in 1951—see if they can be spotted! *(Date: 29 May 1985.)*

42
Chilcompton Tunnel
(183 ST 652 522)

BR Class '4' 4-6-0 No 75007, carrying a temporary shed plate on the smoke box, having recently been allocated to Templecombe, bursts from the 66-yard Chilcompton Tunnel with the 16.37 'Down' stopping train from Bath. Note the patchwork quilt effect on the portals' facing—achieved accidentally by the use of different materials to repair them. *(Photo: Ivo Peters. Date: 14 September 1963.)*

A photographer does his best to please his public! Note the late afternoon shadow cast across the 'Up' portal even appears the same! It is now used as a 25-yard range by the Midsomer Norton and District Rifle Club. The 'Down' portal is used as a farm storage shed. A driveway has been made from the road above and the area is kept clean and tidy. *(Date: 12 March 1985.)*

Map 11, 1904: Chilcompton

Chilcompton is situated high above the valley where part of the village lies. It was an oasis for banking engines to replenish their water supplies before returning to Radstock. Chilcompton had a large water tower situated behind the station buildings. The station was close to Downside School and was used for special trains to run to and from London via Templecombe at the beginning and end of terms.

The sidings were used to handle coal brought down from New Rock Colliery situated a half mile distant from the station. Only the 'Down' platform survives today.

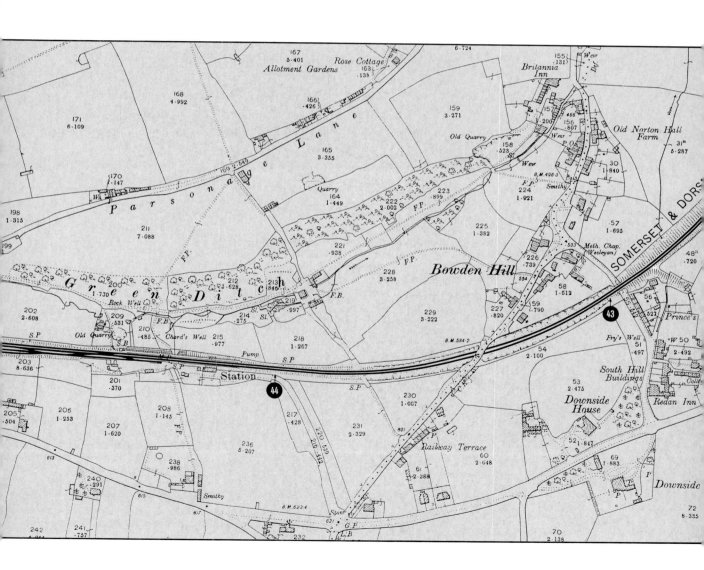

43
Chilcompton 'Rock Cutting' and Bridge No 51
(183 ST 649 515)

Swinging round the curve on Chilcompton Bank, BR Class '4' 2-6-0 No 76006 brings the 13.10 Bath-Bournemouth train over the bridge just before it enters 'Rock Cutting' near Chilcompton Station. The twin portals of Chilcompton Tunnel are visible in the distance.

In the foreground stand concrete tank traps placed at strategic points down the line in 1940. Note the photographer's shadow! *(Photo: Tony Wadley. Date: 28 December 1965.)*

The scene has remained virtually unchanged—a little dreaming and one can imagine new ballast and track being laid here again, quite easily! The ugly corrugated iron parapet top is as much an eyesore today as it was then. Note Chilcompton Tunnel in the background (left)—with a patch over one of its eyes! *(Date: 1 May 1985.)*

44
Chilcompton Station (183 ST 645 514)

BR Class '4' 2-6-0 No 76006 from the Eastleigh Shed gets under way from Chilcompton Station with the 13.10 'Up' stopping train from Bournemouth West.

Ivo Peters' midnight blue Bentley stands on the station road in front of the buildings. The water tower seen in the background was used extensively by banking engines before returning to Radstock. Notice the steepness of the valley on the side of which the station was built. *(Photo: Ivo Peters. Date: 14 September 1963.)*

I am afraid I cannot match the elegance of Ivo Peters' Bentley, but at least I have tried to park in the same spot! The kerb seen in the original photograph was actually a white painted rail section let into the surface. This I found, and it provided a good reference point as little else remains of Chilcompton Station, apart from the 'Down' platform. The area had been vacated by Sheppards Saw Mills which closed recently. Some of the old machinery can be spotted on the platform which was covered with pieces of dunnage. *(Date: 30 May 1985.)*

45
Moorewood (183 ST 630 511)

The worst of the climb to the summit of the Mendips was over once this bridge had been passed, although it was still mostly uphill all the way to Masbury, the gradient would be no more than 1:63. Nevertheless Driver Arthur Turner and Fireman Colin Powis would still have to work S&D '7F' No 53807 hard to elevate the 08.55 'Down' goods from Bath to the summit, about 2½ miles away, reached beyond Binegar. *(Photo: Ivo Peters. Date: 28 September 1963.)*

This location has been used for selective tipping over recent years—now almost completed—so hopefully this frightful mess will be tidied up soon. The line of railway fence on the 'Down' side is the only railway artefact visible. The line of trees in the background identifies the area.

Whilst taking this photo I was approached by a man on a bicycle. He asked me if I was a member of the Somerset & Dorset Trust—when I replied in the affirmative he said, 'did you know there's a chap producing a book on what the S&D's like now?' 'Well . . .', said I! *(Date: 28 May 1985.)*

46
Between Moorewood and Binegar (183 ST 621 501)

The 15.45 'Down' local goods from Bath hauled by S&D '7F' No 53810 approaches Binegar's 'Down' distant signal which is set 'On'. The signal was constructed from two rail sections bolted together and had an upper quadrant arm which followed S&D/SR design practice, whilst Moorewood's 'Up' distant signal seen on the left was of L&SWR lattice post construction with a lower quadrant arm. Closure of Moorewood's signal box was on 21 June 1965. Bridge No 62 is seen in the background. *(Photo: Ivo Peters. Date: 30 May 1950.)*

The track-bed in this section is remarkable—hardly a weed could be seen in early spring. The ballast, when walked upon, still made a 'crunching' sound, being loosely packed.

The base of the two signals can be seen by a keen eye. A large pebble on the edge of the track in line with the tree in the right foreground, marks the spot where the remains of Binegar's 'Down' distant stood, whilst Moorewood's 'Up' distant base can just be seen under the shadow in the middle distance on the left side of the track-bed between the 'V' of a sapling. **Insert** All that remains of Moorewood's 'Up' distant signal. *(Date: 7 May 1985.)*

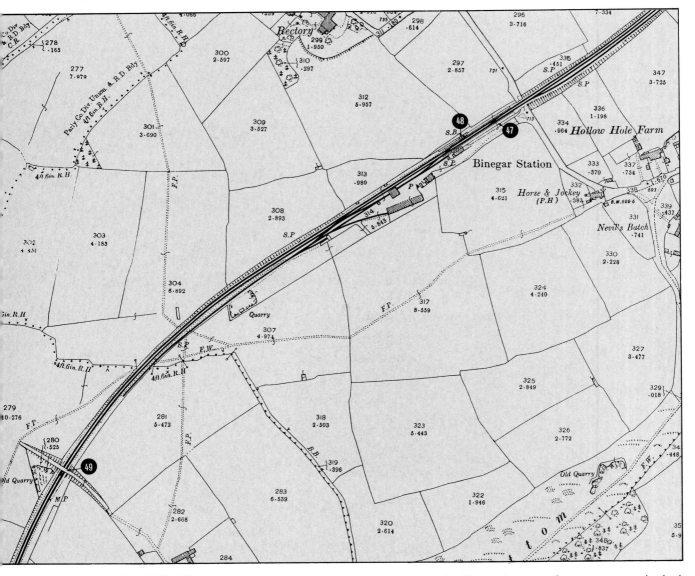

Map 12, 1903: Binegar

Near to the summit of the Mendips was Binegar Station of S&D design.

The siding on the 'Down' side to the north-east was used to transport stone from the quarries at Gurney Slade, being fed by aerial ropeway to a crushing plant adjacent to the railway.

From 1904–21 Oakhill Brewery, famous for its stout, operated a 2ft 6in gauge railway built to transport its product to Binegar from the brewery. Two 0-4-0 tank engines named *Oakhill* and *Mendip* were used for the purpose. It is interesting to note that when this map was published, the year before operations commenced, the narrow gauge railway was not shown! The stone shed at Binegar, often associated with the Oakhill Brewery, is shown on the map as a goods shed served by a siding. Further sidings were subsequently added on the 'Down' side to handle the cattle traffic.

Today the platforms and the station master's house survive and the stone shed is used by a local coal merchant. The nearby Oakhill Manor, which is open to the public, provides continuity in the form of a light railway in its grounds.

47
Binegar (1) (183 ST 616 492)

A double-headed 'Up' local? S&D '7F' No 53804 was coupled ahead of '2P' No 40700 to save having to find a light engine path after taking a freight down to Evercreech from Bath. Binegar was just over a mile from the summit at Masbury, round the bend seen in the distance. A good indication of the line's gradient is seen rising at 1:63 beyond the station. Again the neatness and tidiness of S&D stations can be gauged by the appearance of Binegar in this photograph.

The sturdy signal box doubled as 'Boiland' during the making of a BR instructional film on Emergency Single Line Working in 1956. *(Photo: Ivo Peters. Date: July 1953.)*

What can one say? The platforms are the only reminder of the station seen in this view, although the line formation can be seen. An old loading shovel in the middle distance belongs to the coal merchant now using the stone shed. One recess seen on the 'Up' platform revealed a point rodding bellcrank. The north end of the platforms have been made into a garden for an adjoining bungalow near the road bridge. *(Date: 14 June 1985.)*

48
Binegar (2) (183 ST 616 492)

'There I was at 800ft, and nothing on the clock.' So the driver of Bulleid Pacific No 34041 *Wilton* could have said when recounting the tale. Nearing Masbury Summit on the line's busiest day of the year, *Wilton* with a 'Down' train had dire trouble with her chain-driven valve gear and could not move in either direction. The Binegar station master, Norman Down, rapidly organized rescue by arranging for the pilot engine of the following express to draw *Wilton* and her train back down to Binegar. *Wilton* was shunted ignominiously into a siding to await a fitter to arrive from Bath to 'fix' her up before being towed back to Bath by Stanier 'Black Five' No 44839, seen pictured here later in the day. In the meantime the pilot engine had taken *Wilton*'s train on down the line to Bournemouth. This episode cost over an hour's delay and caused chaos to the crossing schedules on the single line sections!

'Station House' is seen behind the engines together with the stone shed into which ran the light railway from Oakhill Brewery. *(Photo: Ivo Peters. Date: 1 August 1953.)*

Midsomer Norton – Binegar

Late afternoon's sun on a glorious spring day highlights the front of 'Station House' in which the retired station master Norman Down still lives. He was station master for 22 years, from 1944–66. A fine gentleman, who still takes pride in his productive garden, I like to think of him as Binegar's 'sentinel'. Note the old stone shed, now used as a coal yard, also the remains of the platforms.

Right A hand-operated crane still visible in the stone goods shed. *(Date: 28 May 1985.)*

49
Whitnell Farm—Bridge No 66
(183 ST 611 489)

Nearly there! Large-boilered S&D '7F' No 53807, with driver Horace Clarke in charge, approaches Bridge No 66 at Whitnell Farm, near Binegar, with a 'Down' goods assisted by 'Jinty' '3F' 0-6-0T No 47557 at the rear. Only a mile to go to Masbury Summit, then No 47557 will return 'wrong line' to Binegar, having seen the goods safely over the summit. *(Photo: Ivo Peters. Date: 15 March 1952.)*

The only sign left is the 'Up' side fence! A better view of Binegar Church can be seen in this photograph, obscured by steam in Ivo's photo. The farm bridge from which the 1952 photograph was taken has been demolished completely—only a rail-sectioned fence support remains. I had a bovine audience which was intrigued at my balancing on a pair of high steps with camera held aloft to get this shot!
Above right My intrigued audience, clearly unimpressed by the noble history of the fence support which formed part of the division that separated them from my precarious perch. *(Date: 7 May 1985.)*

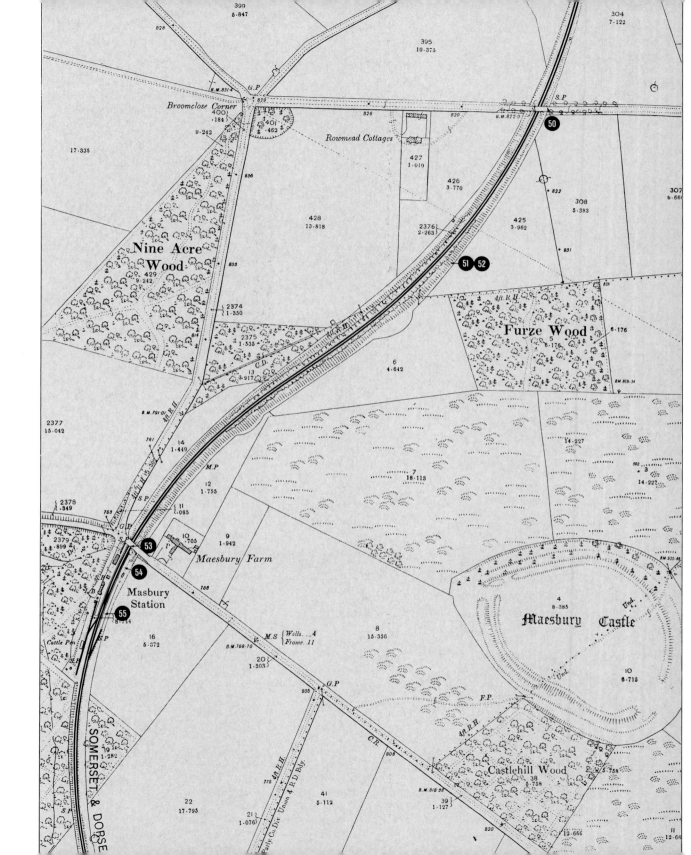

Chapter 5
Masbury— Winsor Hill

Map 13, 1903: Masbury

The summit of the S&D's climb to the Mendips at 811ft above mean sea level was reached in the deep cutting between Nine Acre Wood and Furze Wood.

Today the cutting abounds with saplings. Masbury Station is used as a private dwelling and remains remarkably intact, with the exception of the signal box which has been demolished and replaced by an extension to the station house. The platforms and track-bed between have been laid out to form an attractive garden.

The station never enjoyed great use, but during the Second World War a US Army camp was built nearby and sidings were extended to serve it.

50
Masbury Summit (1)
(183 ST 609 479)

A Bath to Bournemouth excursion nears Masbury Summit, with BR Class '5' No 73051 in charge, on the final stretch of 1:73 gradient, about to pass under Bridge No 69 which carries the B3155 road. Note that some passengers' passion for catching smuts and flies in their faces is being satisfied! *(Photo: Ivo Peters. Date: 7 June 1965.)*

When I first revisited the area shortly after the infilling during the bad winter of 1983, the area resembled the Somme! The area is beginning to recover and will eventually blend into the landscape once more. The farmer may even apply to have a small caravan parking facility here, which provokes the thought that 'S&D Nostalgic Holidays Ltd' could be based here!

Note how the ash tree on the left has grown in twenty years. The track-bed in the distance is still in reasonable condition as are Bridge Nos 68 and 67 further up the track. Just north of this site was a small prefabricated concrete hut about the size of a telephone box on the 'Down' side, which was probably the fogman's hut. *(Date: 7 May 1985.)*

51
Masbury Summit (2)
(183 ST 609 477)

The date—8 September 1962. Worked at 55 per cent cut off and with 240 lb pressure showing on the gauge, Peter Smith takes BR '9F' No 92220, *Evening Star*, on the last 'Up' 'Pines Express' over Masbury Summit, 811' AMSL. At 426 tons it was the heaviest load ever taken over the Mendips unassisted—a marvellous tribute to the crew and the power of the magnificent '9's. It is no wonder that Fireman Aubrey Punter, leaning out of the cab, looks all in as he takes a welcome breather from his efforts!

The summit, on a level stretch of 110 ft was reached around the bend in the foreground and was 435 ft north of the 17½ milepost which can be discerned at the trackside, opposite the first coach. *(Photo: Ivo Peters. Date 8 September 1962.)*

Saplings abound in the deep sided cutting—a few sleepers remain. Foxes have made a home high up the embankment, between some rocks. Notice the outcrop on the right of the photograph—identifiable as that in the original.

In order to stand on this spot well over half an hour's bramble cutting had to be undertaken. In my scramble to leave this location, I lost a foot off my tripod and nearly one of mine when I fell down an old fox hole that was overgrown with brambles! *(Date: 7 May 1985.)*

52
Masbury Summit (3)
(183 ST 609 477)

Peter Smith and Aubrey Punter have
spotted Ivo Peters, both giving him a
friendly wave as BR '9F' 92220,
Evening Star, takes the last 'Up'
'Pines Express' under Bridge 69
towards Binegar and Bath. Notice
the apparent emptiness of the
tender. *(Photo: Ivo Peters. Date: 8
September 1962.)*

The track-bed is still reasonable,
but Bridge 69 has long since gone. It
was removed some time ago as
being 'unsafe'. The B3155 road was
levelled out; so much so that when I
first visited the area, I went straight
past, as at first glance there was no
obvious sign that a railway bridge
once existed here. Only on looking
carefully did I notice the old concrete posts to the north side and
also the cutting on the south side,
which has been backfilled to an
extent of 150 ft or so, as can be seen
in this photograph. *(Date: 7 May
1985.)*

53
Masbury Station (1)
(183 ST 604 473)

Masbury Station was the highest on the Mendips and only served a scattered rural community. This 1937 view shows clearly the unusual layout of the station buildings. The station master's house is situated at the far end of the 'Up' platform; the waiting rooms and booking office are just seen on the right. The small signal box stood on the 'Up' platform and when the station was reduced to a halt in 1935, it closed at night.

The stone crushing plant on the left was built by Mendipadam, a subsidiary of Emborough Stone Company, but was not used to any great degree. By the Second World War it had been demolished and its sidings, seen in the background, were extended to serve a nearby US Army depot. Note the workmen repairing the cinder platform surface. *(Photo: H. C. Casserley. Date: 23 July 1937.)*

Taken from Bridge No 70, the station is readily identifiable, although by summer the same view would be obscured by trees. Note the new extension to 'Station House'. 'Up' trains starting from here faced an immediate 1:50 climb from the platform. *(Date: 9 April 1985.)*

54
Masbury Station (2)
(183 ST 604 473)

The 'Up' 'Pines Express' piloted by
'2P' No 40700 and a BR Class '5',
pass Masbury Station on the final
stretch of the north-bound climb to
the summit, ¼ mile away. Note the
cinder surface of the platforms
which were built of compacted clay
with a brick face. The tall 'Down'
starting signal is clearly seen on the
left. *(Photo: Lens of Sutton. Date:
late 1950s.)*

Mr Wilfred Couling, who was relief
station master at Evercreech Junction, has lived here since 1954,
when trains still stopped at the halt.
He has made the station platforms
and track-bed into an attractive
garden by planting a variety of trees,
which is undertaken with difficulty
as every hole has to be dug into the
ballast and compacted chippings.
   I was talking to Mr Couling about
Ivo Peters' prowess in racing trains
up the Mendips, enabling several
photographs to be taken of the
same train at different locations.
'One could do that,' he said. He
then told me how he could leave
Evercreech Junction at the same
time as 'The Pines', by car or motor-
cycle, and on the way home watch
the train slowly going over Prestleigh Viaduct and on to Cannards
Grave. He arrived home at Masbury,
put his car in the garage, walked to
the platform to hear the train still
some way off, climbing the 1:50
gradient up to the station! *(Date: 9
April 1985.)*

55
Masbury Station (3)
(183 ST 604 472)

The passengers on the Warwick-
shire Railway Society's special had
a lot to complain about. The
weather was foul and Masbury Summit was enveloped in thick cloud,
thus restricting what should have
been splendid views of the countryside. In addition, the 'imported' BR
'9F' No 92238's performance that
day was abysmal, the climb to the
summit of the Mendips at times at
no more than a snail's pace! However, 92238 has a chance to regain
some of her steam as she drifts
under Bridge No 70 past Masbury
Halt's 'Down' platform.

It was very difficult to hear trains
approaching from the north, as they
passed under this bridge, having
built up speed on the ¼ mile run
downhill from the summit. Wilfred
Couling states that somewhere
between twenty and thirty farm cats
were killed this way having failed to
hear trains coming! *(Photo: The late
Derek Cross, via D. M. Cross. Date:
12 June 1965.)*

The spring blossom out on the
young trees planted on the station
platforms and the track-bed provide
a dramatic contrast. 'Station House'
is a constant reminder of the area's
past history. Some people have
wandered around here looking at
the old station, completely over-
looking the fact that it is a private
dwelling and garden, which is very
disconcerting to Wilfred Couling
and his wife. *(Date: 7 May 1985.)*

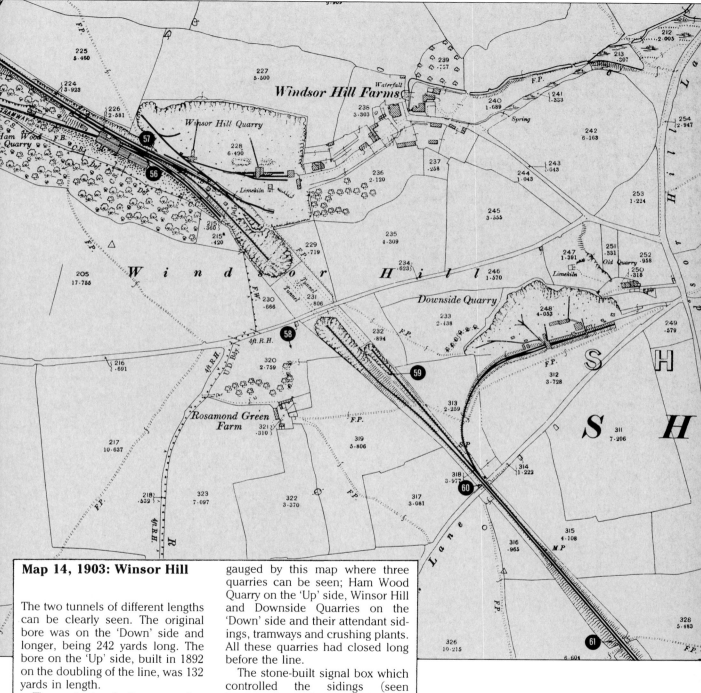

Map 14, 1903: Winsor Hill

The two tunnels of different lengths can be clearly seen. The original bore was on the 'Down' side and longer, being 242 yards long. The bore on the 'Up' side, built in 1892 on the doubling of the line, was 132 yards in length.

The extent of the quarrying industry on the Mendips can be gauged by this map where three quarries can be seen; Ham Wood Quarry on the 'Up' side, Winsor Hill and Downside Quarries on the 'Down' side and their attendant sidings, tramways and crushing plants. All these quarries had closed long before the line.

The stone-built signal box which controlled the sidings (seen between the tracks just north of the tunnels) closed in 1948.

56
Ham Wood Quarry sidings
(183 ST 612 452)

BR Class '4' 2-6-0 No 76019 passes Ham Wood sidings with an 'Up' train, having just emerged from the 132 yard 'new' Winsor Hill Tunnel. Notice the fence separating the sidings from the main line. The quarry and stone crushing plant which they served closed shortly after World War 2 and have long since been disused. The connecting points were removed when the track on the main line was replaced. *(Photo: Tony Wadley. Date: 11 December 1965.)*

Only the indentations of sleepers from the sidings now mark this spot. The track-bed is still in good condition, being regularly used by farmers and walkers. Remains of the Ham Wood stone crushing plant can be seen. Various pieces of twisted corrugated iron, an old water tank and stonework lie scattered at the track side. Somebody has taken the trouble to tow a car right up here and dumped it next to the old stone crushing plant. *(Date: 28 May 1985.)*

Left A little further up the line, Ham Wood Viaduct spans a ravine and remains in very good condition, despite being almost totally obscured by trees.

57
Winsor Hill Tunnel (north portal) (183 ST 613 452)

The 'Up' 'Pines Express' hauled by '2P' 4-4-0 No 40697 and Bulleid Pacific No 34042, *Dorchester*, emerges from the north end of the 132 yard tunnel, built when the line was doubled in 1892. This was shorter than the original bore, seen on the left, which was 242 yards in length. During the construction of the first tunnel four navvies lost their lives in a rockfall. They lie buried in the cemetery at Shepton Mallet.

The stone signal box, the only one on the line, was closed in August 1948, after the closure of Ham Wood and Winsor Hill sidings. Notice how the line diverges to pass either side of the box to and from the tunnel. *(Photo: Ivo Peters. Date: 18 September 1954.)*

The tunnel mouths appear overgrown in this shot, however the 'Up' portal remains clear and can easily be seen further round the bend. It stands open-mouthed as if expectantly awaiting the next train to pass through. Its condition remains good. The 'Down' tunnel is sinister by comparison and is somewhat overgrown. Its portals are covered by massive steel doors which were put there by Rolls-Royce in 1968, who used the tunnel for destructive tests on the Olympus jet engine for Concorde. They ran the engine without oil, expecting it to 'blow' within twenty minutes or so—in the event it actually ran for well over two hours! The period of use was only for a few days, planning permission having been sought previously from Shepton Mallet RDC as a matter of course, in case an explosion caused a change in the local topography! *(Date: 28 May 1985.)*

Left The north portal of Winsor Hill 'Up' Tunnel. *(Date: 28 May 1985.)*

58
Winsor Hill (183 ST 613 450)

A '7F' 2-8-0 toils northbound on the 1:50 gradient towards Winsor Hill Tunnel with an evening goods. This view from Winsor Hill summarizes the pastoral pleasures of the S&D enjoyed by the lineside photographer. *(Photo: Ivo Peters. Date: 29 September 1956.)*

With a flask of coffee at my side, I took a welcome break from the exertions of a hard day's photography and lay back on the hillside to doze, reflecting on the scenes of yesteryear. It is incredible today to think of this area bearing witness to the sight and sounds of heavy trains pounding up the southern slopes of the Mendips, their exhausts echoing in the tunnel cuttings at the base of the hillside. '*So I awoke, and behold it was a dream.*' John Bunyan (1628–88). *(Date: 28 May 1985.)*

59
Winsor Hill Tunnel (south)
(1) (183 ST 616 449)

S&D '7F' No 53805 emerges out of the 'Down' portal of Winsor Hill Tunnel with the 10.45 'Down' coal train from Midsomer Norton (Norton Hill Colliery). It will be braking most of the way to Charlton Road Viaduct at Shepton Mallet, some 1½ miles away, before opening up to climb the 1:55 gradient to Shepton Mallet Station. The guard in his van will have his brake applied at the rear of the train, helping to control the descent. The braking properties of the '7F's were excellent—partly due to their being fitted with Ferodo brake blocks. *Photo: Ivo Peters. Date: 27 March 1954.)*

The tunnel mouth is now obscured by trees. On my first visit here the cutting was littered with polythene and paper blown down from the tip at the top of the hill in the disused Downside Quarry. Now the tip has closed and the area has been cleaned up. Notice the one solitary post showing on the bank! *(Date: 28 May 1985.)*

60
Winsor Hill Tunnel (south) (2)
(183 ST 616 448)

BR Class '9F' No 92212 drifts out of Winsor Hill Tunnel towards the small bridge (No 78) over Forum Lane with the 09.35 (SO) Sheffield to Bournemouth train.

The catch points on the left were to deal with any 'breakaways' from goods trains on the 1:50 gradient. Until 1940 there was a siding controlled by a ground frame (the key to which was collected from Winsor Hill Box) to Downside Quarry (on the hill), the trailing points of which left the main line to the front of the '9F'. Note how the lines diverged to enter the tunnels. *(Photo: Ivo Peters. Date: 26 August 1961.)*

The trees are easily identifiable although grown. The track-bed is distinct and used for occasional grazing. Walkers from Shepton Mallet frequently use this area. The base of the permanent way hut can still be seen, plus rubble. A sign of the times adorns the bridge here—a CND symbol!

The day of my visit the weather was glorious—not a cloud in the sky! *(Date: 28 May 1985.)*

61

Bridge 79 (between Winsor Hill and Shepton Mallet)
(183 ST 618 446)

A fine study of SR Pacifics Nos 34006, *Bude*, (with Donald Beale in control) and 34057, *Biggin Hill*, as they climb up the 1:50 gradient towards Winsor Hill, with a LCGB excursion, which was one of the last trains to travel the line.

It was Saturday 5 March 1966—the sun shome brilliantly on the pen-ultimate day that trains were to run over the S&D. On Sunday, the weather was dull and overcast, reflecting the sombre mood of many people that day. Note the branches of saplings just visible on the right. *(Photo: David Milton. Date: 5 March 1966.)*

The same scene today, which just goes to show how things grow in a short period of time. This photograph, taken in a howling westerly gale, vividly illustrates the point. The bridge parapet can just be made out through the thicket. Note also the post in the centre! *(Date: 30 April 1985.)*

Midford Valley
(172 ST 762 602)

BR Class '5' No 73051 sweeps round
the bend from Midford with a
'Down' express on a glorious
summer's day. Note the high retaining wall under which used to be a
short siding. Midford Castle can be
seen on the hill in the background.
*(Photo: R. C. Riley (5498). Date:
12 August 1961.)*

Autumn berries adorn the bushes in
the beautiful Midford Valley. The
reluctant sun peeps through the
clouds to ensure that the full rich-
ness of the autumn colours are
highlighted in this tranquil setting.
(Date: 5 October 1985.)

Above Soon after the formation of
the Joint line in 1875, the crest,
which combined the arms of Bath
and the seal of Dorchester, was
available for use on the sides of
locomotives and carriage stock. It
was worn until the major railway
company reforms of 1930.

Wellow Valley
(172 ST 731 571)

Class '9F' 2-10-0 No 92001 passes through the lovely Wellow Valley with a 'Down' express. Seen in the distance is St Julian's Church in the village of Wellow. *(Photo: R. C. Riley (5507). Date: 12 August 1961.)*

Today a large poultry unit has been built on the track-bed in the middle distance. The embankment of the line formation gives a clue as to the location, as does Wellow Church. Note how the tree on the left has grown! *(Date: 5 October 1985.)*

Radstock (North) 'A' Signal box (172/183 ST 693 550)

Dick Riley enjoys a footplate ride on a '7F' hauling an 'Up' goods and has a splendid view of the tall Radstock (North) 'A' box. Note the parapets of the demolished 'Marble Arch' and 'new' Tyning bridge. *(Photo: R. C. Riley (6429). Date: 26 June 1962.)*

Today the parapets are still quite distinctive, as is the old tree-covered slag heap in the background. Note the crane working on Writhlington Colliery's slag heap in the distance. *(Date: 5 October 1985.)*

Midsomer Norton
(183 ST 664 537)

Class '7F' No 53810, face to face
with '3F' 47316, gets under way from
Midsomer Norton with an 'Up'
goods. Note Norton Hill Colliery
sidings in the background. *(Photo:
R. C. Riley (5721). Date: 3 July
1961.)*

The afternoon sun appears briefly
from behind the clouds to shine on
the old station building, now in the
process of being renovated. *(Date:
5 October 1985.)*

Chapter 6
Shepton Mallet—Evercreech

Map 15, 1903: Shepton Mallet

The S&D crossed over two viaducts in Shepton Mallet, the Bath Road Viaduct (118 yards) and the Charlton Viaduct, (317 yards) and clearly visible on the map.

The layout was quite extensive at Shepton Mallet. The 'Down' yard contained sidings serving a stone crushing plant and an adjacent quarry producing ballast for the railway. The S&D passed under the East Somerset line of the GWR, connecting Yatton and Witham, through two distinctly different bridge arches! Also of interest is the Charlton Lime Works on the 'Up' side. Today the whole site is covered by an industrial estate.

62
Shepton Mallet—(Charlton Road) (183 ST 628 431)

BR Class '9F' No 92006 with the 07.43 (SO) Bradford to Bournemouth coasting over the curved 27-arch Charlton Road Viaduct and the A361 road bridge, nears Shepton Mallet Station, where she was booked to stop.

The Charlton Road Viaduct was unusual in so far as the line dipped at 1:55 to the centre and then changed to a 1:55 gradient up. This enabled trains to take a 'good run at it' to aid the climb up the opposite side.

Note the tall 'Up' advanced starting signal which could be seen from the bridges to the south of the station. The small 'Down' goods yard is on the right of the photograph, which was taken from the station footbridge. (Photo: Ivo Peters. Date: 5 August 1961.)

One of the dramatically different scenes of today. The area has been developed into an industrial estate. The unit in the foreground is a meat packing plant. I was very fortunate in being able to take this photograph with the kind assistance of the staff of Tachograph Services, who hoisted me 16 ft in the air on a fork-lift truck! Fortunately the area in the foreground was not blocked with lorries, enabling Charlton Road Viaduct to be seen in the distance. Showerings, the manufacturers of Babycham and part of Allied Breweries, paid BR £5 for it in 1971 and have spent over £30,000 on it in the last five or six years, including £13,500 recently tarmacing the surface.

Left Charlton Road Viaduct from Showerings gardens. *(Date: 17 June 1985.)*

63
Shepton Mallet (Charlton Road) Station (183 ST 629 430)

The powerful combination of S&D '7F' No 53808 piloting BR Class '5' No 73047 with the 09.25 (SO) Bournemouth to Manchester and Liverpool, passes Shepton Mallet Station. Notice the bridges in the background being totally different in design, a legacy of the doubling of the line in 1892. The goods shed and 'Up' yard can be seen in the background behind the train. This photograph was taken from the signal box on the 'Down' platform. *(Photo: Ivo Peters. Date: 1 September 1962.)*

The only immediate similarities are the twin bridges in the background and the cottage on the left! The small 'village' of Portacabins is being used by the Gas Corporation as an HQ for the laying of a major pipeline in the region.

My perching on tiptoes from the top of a tall pair of steps, taking this photograph, brought looks of incredulity from observers in the industrial unit behind me. 'What's that for then?' 'Nice shot of a picturesque view' I replied! *(Date: 16 May 1985.)*

Left View of Shepton Mallet Station taken from the footbridge looking south. Notice the steam rising from carriage in the background after a shower! *(Photo: D. Milton. Date: summer 1961.)*

64
Shepton Mallet (Charlton Road) Station (183 ST 629 429)

BR Class '4' 2-6-0 No 76015, coupled ahead of BR Class '9F' 2-10-0 No 92220, *Evening Star*, to save a light engine working down to Evercreech Junction, gets away from Shepton Mallet with the 09.03 Bristol to Bournemouth train.

The stone-built goods shed can be seen on the left. The signal box, footbridge and water tower are seen on the right. *(Photo: Ivo Peters. Date: 1 September 1962.)*

The old bacon factory chimney provides an identifiable link with the previous photograph (partly obscured by steam)—otherwise one would have a job to know! Contractors' vehicles and a Portacabin stand where the Class '4' was seen! *(Date: 16 May 1985.)*

65
Shepton Mallet goods yard
(183 ST 628 428)

The low sun on a winter's afternoon accentuates the sturdy lines of S&D Class '7F' No 53803, as she collects some coal trucks from Shepton Mallet's yard before proceeding to Midsomer Norton with the 13.45 'Up' goods (from Evercreech). Note the Great Western cattle truck in the background. *(Photo: Ivo Peters. Date: 23 February 1952.)*

The culprit caught! The crane seems to be wearing an odious smile as it occupies the spot where the '7F' once stood. This piece of contractor's plant was responsible for at least twenty or thirty minutes delay when photographing the bridge behind because the jib blocked the view of chimneys I wished to use as identification points!

Note the cottage roof on the left—identifiable as being that in the original photograph. *(Date: 16 May 1985.)*

66
Shepton Mallet, GWR
Witham Branch
(183 ST 629 426)

0-6-0PT No 9615 with a pick-up goods from Witham to Wells on the GWR Witham to Yatton Branch crosses over the S&D just south of Shepton Mallet Station. Note the two distinctly different bridges. The chimney on the left is of an old lime works, whilst the one next to the water tower was a bacon factory. *(Photo: R. E. Toop. Date: 31 March 1959.)*

The area of the track-bed has been made into a small industrial estate which has a dozen or more units; further units are in the process of being built.

This is just another example of the many dramatic changes that have taken place. The two bridges, now used as a builder's store, provide a tentative link with the past. Note the distant Mendip Hills, over which the S&D had to pass. *(Date: 1 July 1985.)*

67
Cannards Grave
(183 ST 629 413)

The charm and variety of locomotives and rolling stock can be gauged by this photograph. Large-boilered S&D '7F' No 53806 nears Cannards Grave with the 12.20 (SO) relief, Bournemouth to Walsall, made up of ten ex-LNER coaches. This was a heavy load for the '7F' to take over the Mendips unassisted.

Whitstone Hill Farm is set high on the hill to the left and at night driver Donald Beale was able to use its light as a landmark to gauge his position! *(Photo: Ivo Peters. Date: 15 August 1953.)*

The area has been completely filled in with non toxic materials and builders' rubble from here right to the location of the ex-roadbridge near the GWR Witham Branch. Over forty acres of land have been reclaimed and turned back to pasture and arable land. The local landowner/farmer is Chris Norman, whose great-grandfather, Richard Norman, farmed here when the railway went through, the Norman family, having farmed in the area since the 1820s. Interesting comparisons were made between the manpower needed to excavate the deep cutting, which was over a mile long, and the amount of horsepower used by bulldozers and mechanical loaders to fill it back in!

The two electricity poles provide a reference point as do the trees in the background. *(Date: 17 June 1985.)*

68
Prestleigh Viaduct
(183 ST 633 406)

Class '4F' 0-6-0 No 44561 crawls over Prestleigh Viaduct up the 1:50 gradient with an Evercreech—Bath goods. Sometimes the forward movement of such trains was barely discernible on the severe gradients! The eleven arches of the viaduct are shown to good advantage in this splendid view. *(Photo: Ivo Peters. Date: April 1955.)*

When is the next train due? It is hard to see from this photograph that some twenty years have passed since the structure bore the weight of a locomotive! This is an example of how some scenes appear time-less. Sheep graze in the fields above and below the viaduct, whilst cloud shadows steal over the hills in the background.

'And did those feet in ancient time
Walk upon England's mountains
*   green?*
And was the Holy Lamb of God
On England's pleasant pastures
*   seen?'*
Wm Blake (1757–1827)
(Date: 30 April 1985.)

Map 16, 1903: Evercreech New

This station once handled consider-able milk traffic and lime from various works which were located near the line and one can be seen on the map. The station was con-veniently placed on the edge of this large village, albeit fairly modest itself in size. Today the station site has been built upon with modern housing.

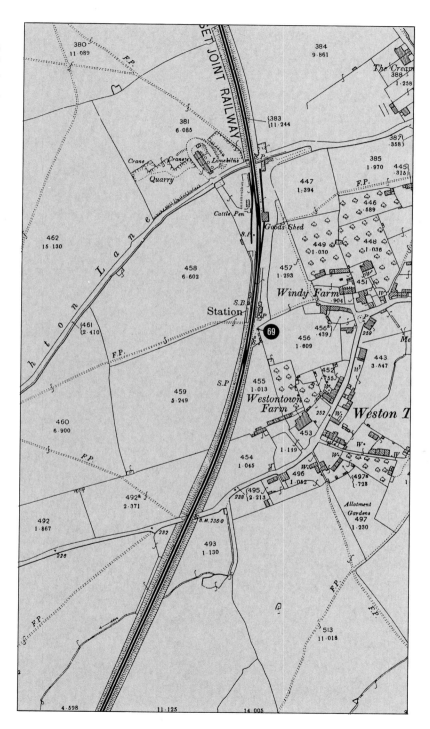

69
Evercreech New
(183 ST 645 386)
Evercreech New, situated on the western edge of the village, enjoys a quiet moment on a summer's afternoon. Station master Reg Jeans, seen standing in the field on the right, was actually playing cricket with two small boys!

The layout of this attractive station can be judged well from this photograph, taken from the tall 'Down' starting signal. The edifice on the left is the remains of a lime works and kiln. Note the small but neat goods yard.
(Photo: David Milton. Date: summer 1961.)

I promise you this was once Evercreech New! If it was not for the hill in the background this location would be extremely hard to recognize and is a dramatic contrast to the previous pair of photographs! Some station railings on the left ('Up' side) can still be seen and now form garden boundary fences. The public footpath just seen in the foreground on the original photograph crosses in front of the shiplap fencing. *(Date: 30 April 1985.)*

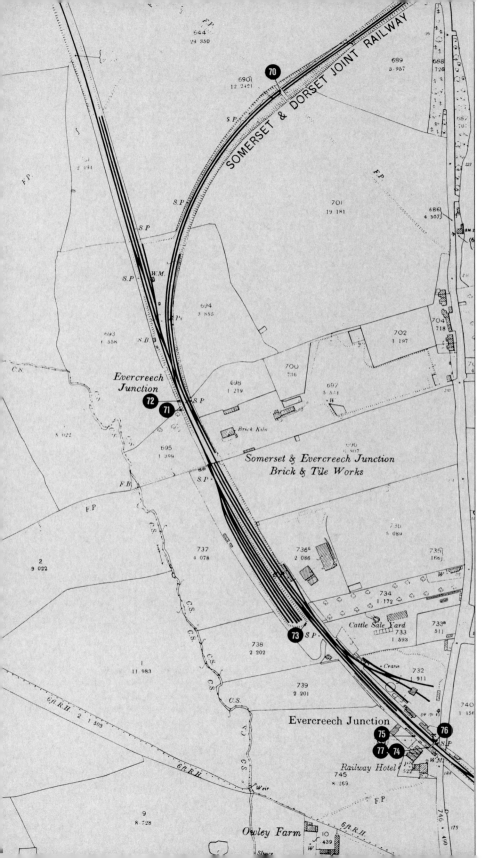

Map 17, 1902: Evercreech Junction

The map clearly shows the sharp curve of the main line as it swings round to join the branch line past the 'North Box' before entering the station. This curve, which had a 25 mph speed restriction, was the start of the S&D's extension to Bath, which was authorized in 1871 and completed in 1874.

Although similar in layout, a few noticeable changes took place at Evercreech Junction after publication of this map. A 56 ft turntable was located between the 'V' of the branch and the main line. It is interesting to note the location of the turntable behind the 'Down' platform on the 1902 map.

The principal goods yard was located on the 'Up' side and served by five sidings. A loop which connected this yard to the branch line, skirting the west side of the north signal box, enabling goods traffic to be handled to and from the branch without having to cross the main lines, was added subsequently. In addition, the 'Down' or 'New' yard adjacent to the branch line was increased to five sidings. The small 'Down' yard behind the station buildings had a goods shed and cattle yards.

All freight trains called at the yards and some started or terminated from here. Shunting was a 24-hour activity. The centre siding in which pilot engines waited to assist heavy trains over the Mendips can be seen between the running lines through the station. Also of interest is the siding built to serve the Somerset & Evercreech Junction Brick & Tile Works.

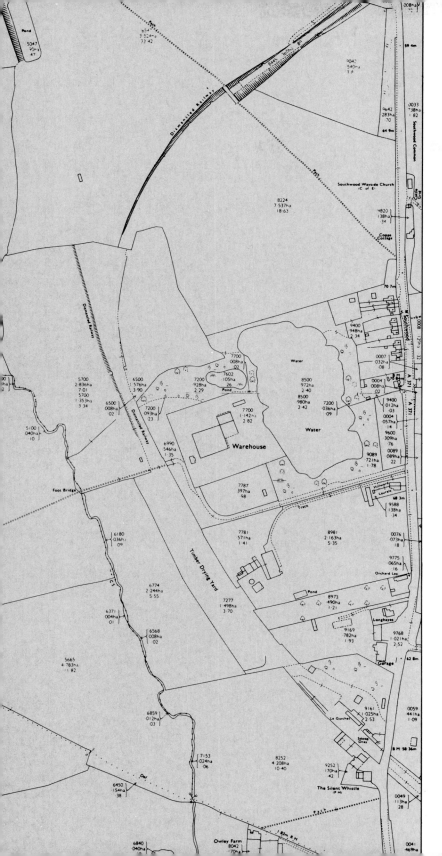

Map 18, 1972: Evercreech Junction

The changes are plain to see—the station buildings on the 'Down' side remain intact and form private dwellings. The site is now a sawmill and timber yard.

The area beyond the timber drying yard, upon which a few small industrial buildings have been built, has been completely returned to agriculture. The only tangible reminder of its railway heritage is the small guards' cabin and mess room still standing all on its own in the middle of a field! (This has been highlighted on the map.)

Also a poignant reminder, probably often repeated around the country, is the old Railway Hotel, appropriately re-named. No prizes for guessing the meaning of 'Le Guichet' and 'Sdoog Dray' as the station buildings are now named! (The first is French for 'booking office', try some reverse thinking for the second!) The large warehouse is Slades, builders' merchants.

70

'North Box' to Pecking Mill Curve (Evercreech Junction)
(183 ST 638 374)

This severe curve had a 25 mph speed restriction and on 'Up' trains required careful handling by such locomotives as the Bulleid Pacifics, which had a propensity to slip.

Seen here is No 34042, *Dorchester*, in charge of the 09.55 (SO) Bournemouth to Leeds piloted by '4F' 0-6-0 No 44558.

In the background behind the engines is the guards' cabin and mess room adjacent to the 'Down' goods yard, on the Highbridge and Burnham Branch, which is just visible. Note the 'refuge' built into the retaining wall. *(Photo: Ivo Peters. Date: 21 July 1951.)*

Mangles? . . . looks like this building has been through one! If one did not know that a railway used to run through here a few years ago, the building appears ancient!

This untidy scene was taken from an attractive three-arched farm bridge spanning the old line. Note the 'refuge' is still visible just to the right of the building.

Above The guards' cabin and mess room. *(Date: 30 April 1985.)*

71
Evercreech Junction 'North Box' (183 ST 637 370)

A good view of the 32-lever 'North Box' and the branch line to Highbridge and Burnham heading into the distance.

Cautiously negotiating the sharp curve around 'North Box' are '2P' No 40563 and Bulleid Pacific No 34042,

Dorchester, in charge of the 09.40 (SO) Sheffield to Bournemouth. The curve was a legacy of the extension built to Bath in 1874, which diverted from the then main line to Glastonbury and Highbridge. The loop around 'North Box' can be seen to advantage, which meant shunting operations in the 'Up' yard could carry on without encroaching on the main running lines.

Note the calling back signal on the right of the picture; this was used for authorizing 'Down' freight trains to reverse on the 'Down' main line and then back into the 'Up' goods yard adjacent to the branch. 'North Box' was burnt down on the night of 5 March 1966. *(Photo: Ivo Peters. Date: 8 August 1953.)*

'The storm has gone over me, and I lie like one of those old oaks which the late hurricane has scattered about me. I am stripped of all my honours, I am torn up by the roots, *and lie prostrate on the earth!'* Edmund Burke, (1729–97).

What more can one say? *(Date: 15 June 1985.)*

72
Evercreech Junction
(183 ST 637 370)

BR Class '4' 4-6-0 No 75073 on the 'Up Mail' nears 'North Box' and the sharp right hand curve on the start of the 8½-mile climb up the Mendips. The 'Up Mail' had priority over the other traffic on the line and everything was done to ensure no delay occurred and that it arrived on time!

Note the 'calling back' signal seen to the left. Also the 'Up' goods yard in the background. *(Photo: Ivo Peters. Date: 25 July 1964.)*

The building seen through the trees on the left and the distant hills give a clue as to the location, otherwise the area bears little or no relationship to yesterday's scene. Note the small industrial units built on the site of the 'Up' goods yard. *(Date: 15 June 1985.)*

73

Evercreech Junction
(183 ST 639 366)

The classic scene for which the S&D will be remembered best. The 8½ mile assault of the Mendips is about to begin. Class '2P' No 40568 and 'Black Five' No 44839 blast away from Evercreech Junction on the 1:105 gradient to take the 09.25 (SO) Bournemouth to Manchester and Liverpool train northwards.

Over the train two pilot engines can be seen waiting in the centre siding to take their turn to assist heavy trains up the Mendips. The goods shed and station buildings can be seen in the background. *(Photo: Ivo Peters. Date: 21 July 1951.)*

The sun peeps out from behind the clouds to highlight the old station buildings, on a glorious afternoon in June. This area is now a sawmill. Note the timber stored awaiting preparation in the mill, seen just behind the trees on the left.

The previous vantage point was taken from the bank at the end of the 'Up' sidings. My vantage point was from a box mounted on a fork truck! *(Date: 15 June 1985.)*

74
Evercreech Junction
(183 ST 640 365)

'A sledge hammer to crack a nut!', BR '9F' 92220, *Evening Star*, returns to the S&D for a few months due to the shortage of motive power caused by several locomotives being away and under repair. A request was made for two Class '5's, but Bath received two '9F's instead. The length of the Class '9F's precluded their use on freight trains to Evercreech as they could not be turned on the turntable. Their heavy use of coal on three- or four-coach trains did not help the cost effectiveness on what by now was a purely local service run on the S&D, through traffic having ceased in 1962.

The station layout is seen to good advantage. Note the centre siding in which pilot engines and waiting branch line trains were kept. *(Photo: Ivo Peters. Date: 12 September 1963.)*

With the kind help of Mr and Mrs Nash, who now live at Evercreech Junction, the footbridge was recreated for the day in the shape of a forklift truck fitted with a large box from which I obtained the facsimile of their home! Note the extension built onto the old ticket office on the 'Down' platform. In the distance is the small industrial estate built on the 'Up' goods yard.

When Mrs Nash first saw my car draw up outside her house, the roof-rack laden with ladders and steps, she thought I was a window cleaner and instructed her son to send me away! There was much hilarity when the true reason for my mission was established!

Above right The re-created footbridge with the intrepid photographer aboard. *(Photo: M. J. Arlett. Date: 15 June 1985.)*

75
Evercreech Junction
(183 ST 639 365)

Class '3F' 0-6-0 43218 arrives with a stopping train from Highbridge, bringing it to a halt in front of the level crossing over the A371 road. The footbridge and large water tower can be observed. The tall 'Down' starting signal's post over the chimney of the engine can also be seen.

The 'Up' platform, from which this photograph was taken, appears to be neat and tidy as one would expect of an S&D station. The staff always had a generous supply of magazines in the waiting rooms—a nice gesture that typified the attitude of S&D railway folk. *(Photo: R. E. Toop. Date: 1 June 1957.)*

A garage has been built on the 'Up' platform, but 'Sdoog Dray' remains unaltered by the change! The track-bed between the platforms has been filled to form a lawn. The 'Down' platform edge can still be seen. *(Date: 15 June 1985.)*

76
Evercreech Junction
(183 ST 640 365)

Mr O. S. Nock, the well-known railway author, points out the line of pilot engines standing in the middle road to his wife. Evercreech Junction on a Saturday was a mecca for steam enthusiasts to savour the tremendous variety of sight and sound that it could offer. The steep gradient up from the station can be judged by the sidings in the background being on level ground! *(Photo: Ivo Peters. Date: 5 July 1952.)*

The platform is a little cracked now, but still quite distinct. Notice the neatly kept bushes and lawns that now adorn the platforms and track-bed. The garage built on the 'Up' platform can be seen to the left. The station and buildings were put up for tender by BR in 1970. A reply to the newspaper advertisement offering a mere £5,050 secured them!

This photograph was made possible by the use of the fork lift truck placed over the site of the footbridge! *(Date: 15 June 1985.)*

Insert The keeper's cottage at Lamyatt Crossing. *(Date: 8 May 1985.)*

77
Evercreech Junction
(183 ST 640 365)

SR Pacific No 34041, *Wilton*, furiously blowing off at 250 lb per sq inch gets under way with a southbound express for Bournemouth from Evercreech Junction.

A good view of the tall south signal box which housed a 26-lever frame and controlled the crossing over the A371 road seen in the foreground. The large water tower dominates the south view. The line stretches into the distance and on towards Lamyatt Crossing. *(Photo: David Milton. Date: August 1961.)*

A farmer levels out an area of the track-bed in preparation for the erection of a farm building. The base of the old water tower is seen surrounded by bushes. The A371 road is devoid of any railway arte-fact, thus denying the observer any clue as to its past except the old Railway Hotel just to the right of the picture which had been appro-priately re-named 'The Silent Whistle', but which is now called 'The Natterjack'. Slowly but surely the S&D is disappearing into pastoral tranquility. *(Date: 15 June 1985.)*

Chapter 7
Wyke Champflower —Wincanton

78
Wyke Champflower—Bridge No 115 (183 ST 660 344)

This stone bridge was unique as it was built to span double track: all the others on the S&D system were not, being built to span only a single line. When doubled, second spans were built alongside. Popping out from under the bridge is an afternoon local train from Templecombe to Highbridge, with Ivatt 2-6-2T No 41296 in charge. *(Photo: Ivo Peters. Date: 15 May 1965.)*

Like so many bridges on the systems that spanned cuttings, the spans have been used for infilling, as in this case.

This photograph had to be taken in a hurry as there was a boar rapidly closing on me from behind! Mike Arlett was with me as well—he was back over the gate first! *(Date: 1 June 1985.)*

79
Wyke Champflower
(183 ST 661 343)

This is one of my favourite locations on the S&D. Many superb photographs have been obtained near this spot, which is of considerable interest. The sharp curve in the background was the point at which the junction to the GWR line would have been made, a second bridge across Wyke Lane would have been built alongside the existing one (Bridge No 116).

The sharp bend in the line here prevented any fast running, the speed limit being 45 mph around 'Cole Curve' seen in the background. This scene shows Ivatt 2-6-2T No 41216 on an 'Up' local train from Templecombe to Highbridge. *(Photo: The late Derek Cross, via D. M. Cross. Date: 12 June 1965).*

The trees are instantly recognizable although one or two have disappeared, whilst others have 'thinned' somewhat. Note the house extension built back onto the track bed. Bridge 116 in the background is still standing, but only just; the embankments to the south have been cut away and the land turned back to agriculture. Note one of Bruton's many schools' buildings on the horizon. *(Date: 1 June 1985.)*

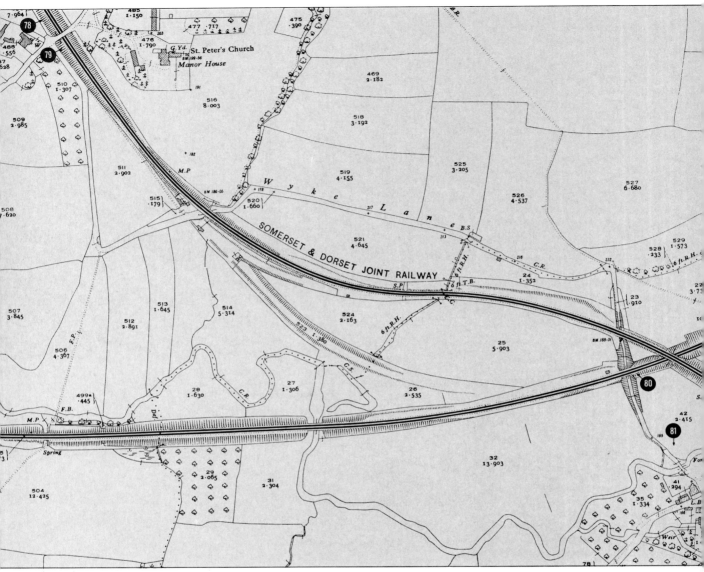

Map 19, 1930: Wyke Champflower

This map is of particular interest because at this point the embankments of the proposed connection to the GWR can be seen. The junction, which apparently was never completed despite much political discussion in the 1860s and 1870s, was to provide a connection between the Bristol and English Channels for the rapid conveyance of the produce from South Wales to ports of the south coast, notably Southampton.

Today all traces of the embankments have disappeared, save a small section, as has much of the S&D line itself between Wyke Lane and the GWR/West of England main line from Paddington, over which it crossed.

80
Cole—Bridge No 118, over the GWR main line
(183 ST 668 339)

This fine study shows the now-preserved WR Castle Class 4-6-0 No 7029, *Clun Castle*, passing under the S&D bridge at Cole with a Paddington-bound express. The driver gives a friendly (?) greeting to Fireman Ron Hyde on the footplate of S&D Class '7F' 2-8-0 No 53805, as it passes over the bridge. It was restarting the 12.20 (SO) Bournemouth to Nottingham train having been stopped by signals at Cole. *(Photo: G. A. Richardson, via Peter Smith. Date: August 1960.)*

How about that? The friendly banter between Mike Arlett and myself on his doubting my ability to recapture the scene is going to cost him another pint! The HST 125 is the 14.25 Plymouth to Paddington. The difference in length between a Castle and an HST power unit minus buffers is about 4 ft 1 in, hence more of the first carriage shows on the HST in my photograph! Note the old bridge parapet now overgrown with ivy. *(Date: 1 June 1985.)*

81
Cole Viaduct (183 ST 668 337)

The cows in the meadow remain oblivious to BR Class '5' No 73068 on the 15.40 'Up Mail' from Bournemouth passing over Cole Viaduct on a beautiful summer's evening.

The five-arched Cole Viaduct spanned the River Brue and a farm track a few yards south from the GW main line. Cole was a train spotter's paradise, as the delights of the S&D could be sampled alongside the GWR by this lovely setting in a valley. *(Photo: Ivo Peters. Date: 31 August 1965.)*

Only the embankment remains—the viaduct blown up.

A month's work of drilling and laying charges culminated in Cole Viaduct being reduced to base material on 12 September 1984. But it still had the last laugh as only 60 per cent of the charges went off, possibly due to air locks in the bore holes. The columns had to be dismantled bit by bit, with a mechanical excavator, the remaining charges being removed by hand pro rata! *(Date: 1 June 1985.)*

Highbridge (182 ST 323 469)

Class '3F' No 43682, which has collected some goods wagons from Highbridge Wharf, crosses over the GW main line and passes the old Highbridge 'A' box. *(Photo: R. C. Riley (2660). Date: 7 July 1959.)*

Half the concrete bridge remains to serve Highbridge's 'Down' platform on the West of England main line. In the immediate foreground the platform has been dug away and I had to stand in the middle of a very prickly bush to obtain this near facsimile! *(Date: 23 September 1985.)*

Bridge 57, near Moorewood
(183 ST 632 513)

2-6-4 T No 80043 draws near Moore-wood and is about to pass under the twin-arch bridge carrying the B3139 road. The worst of the southbound climb of the Mendip Hills was over once this point had been reached. *(Photo: Mrs Angela O'Shea. Date: 31 August 1965.)*

In the paddock formed by the infill-ing of the cutting graze three 'woolly wonders'. The tree line and wall are readily identifiable. The small shed seen on the left of the original picture is extant, but obscured by a small tree. An hour's pause was necessary here to wait for the sun to peep through just enough to allow this photograph to be taken. The bridge has long since been demol-ished, the road levelled and trees planted to form a new hedge line on the north verge. *(Date: 5 October 1985.)*

Moorewood sidings
(183 ST 628 510)

'West Country' Class No 34043 *Combe Martin* pilots BR Class '5MT' No 73051 on the 'Down' 'Pines Express' past the disused Moorewood Colliery sidings. The colliery closed in December 1932. It was served by a light gauge railway (which also incorporated an incline plane up which trucks were winched from the pithead) meeting the S&D system here. The 2ft gauge railway, worked by diminutive 0-6-0 locomotives, was still being used in 1933 for either the transference of coal remaining at the pithead, or for the removal of artefacts still left at the colliery following closure.

This photograph was taken from the embankment of the colliery railway where coal used to be transferred to S&D trucks in the sidings below, probably by the use of chutes.

No 34043 was reputed to be an erratic steamer and one of the less popular members of this class to run over the S&D! *(Photo: R. C. Riley (2949). Date: 5 September 1959.)*

The track-bed has been grassed over and is used as a paddock. The old bridge (No 58) has been demolished, the lane to Downside now passing over an embankment built to replace it. The impressions of the sleepers that once formed the Moorewood Colliery sidings can still be made out, as can the retaining wall of the old embankment of the narrow gauge railway from Moorewood Colliery, which ran parallel to the S&D at this point. Note how little the trees have changed at this location. *(Date: 2 November 1985.)*

Shepton Mallet (Bridge 87)
(183 ST 629 429)

BR Class '4' 2-6-0 No 76015 and BR Class '9F' 2-10-0 No 92220 *Evening Star* head away from Shepton Mallet towards the distinctly different bridges that carry the GWR Wells–Witham branch over the S&D lines.

On this occasion *Evening Star* is being crewed by driver Bill Rawles with fireman Ron Bean, who on 29 March 1960 drove '9F' No 92204 on the first trial of this class to traverse the S&D line. *(Photo: R. C. Riley (6591). Date: 1 September 1962.)*

The cottage and its attendant garden shed provide the immediate clue as to this location.

The debris scattered across the old track-bed remains from a large gas pipeline project which, at the time this photograph was being taken, was largely completed. Only three months earlier the area was a hive of activity with contractors' plant and equipment covering the area of the old Shepton Mallet 'Up' goods yard which is visible in the background.

The bridge over the former 'Up' line in the middle distance has been bricked in on its far side to form a store for a builder's yard. *(Date: 14 November 1985.)*

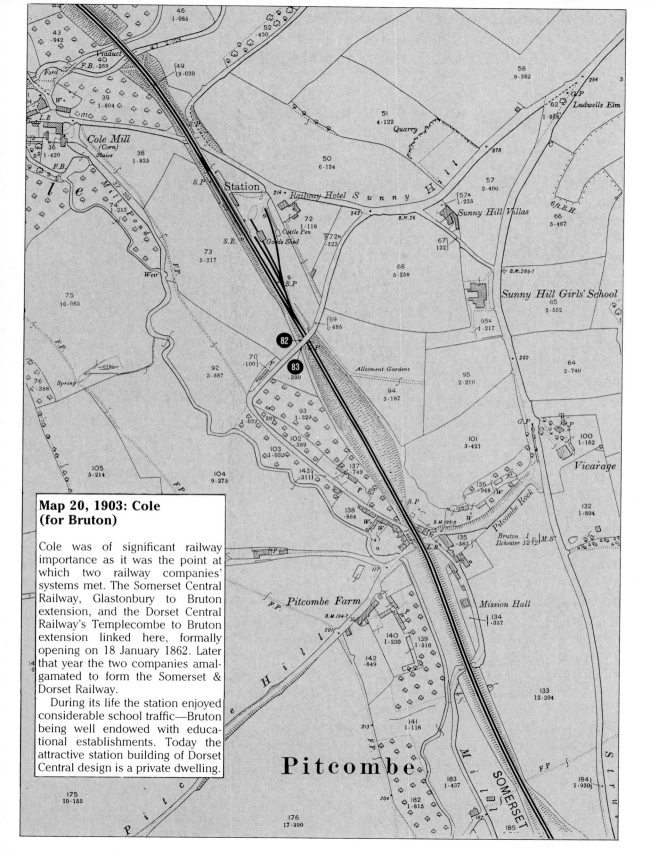

Map 20, 1903: Cole (for Bruton)

Cole was of significant railway importance as it was the point at which two railway companies' systems met. The Somerset Central Railway, Glastonbury to Bruton extension, and the Dorset Central Railway's Templecombe to Bruton extension linked here, formally opening on 18 January 1862. Later that year the two companies amalgamated to form the Somerset & Dorset Railway.

During its life the station enjoyed considerable school traffic—Bruton being well endowed with educational establishments. Today the attractive station building of Dorset Central design is a private dwelling.

82
Cole Station (183 ST 671 334)

An old lady nearing the end of her days, the sole surviving '3F' 0-6-0, Bulldog No 43216, built in 1902 by Neilson, Reid & Co for the S&D (old No 72), sets off from Cole with the 16.00 'Down' local from Highbridge to Templecombe. Less than two months later she was withdrawn. The attractive buildings of Cole Station are evident in this photograph. The building partly obscured by steam was the old Railway Hotel. Note the bridge on the left. *(Photo: The late Derek Cross, via D. M. Cross. Date: 30 June 1962.)*

The sun peeps through scudding clouds casting their shadows on the hills behind, to shine on the buildings of Cole Station and the old Railway Hotel. The track-bed in the foreground has been backfilled to the bridge (No 121) so that only the parapet shows. This was achieved with spoil and rubble removed from Cole Viaduct's demolition. The station building is now an attractive private dwelling, having remained empty for many years.

Whilst photographing the demolition of the viaduct, I met a charming lady whose father was landlord of the Railway Hotel, and she recalled the tale of friendly engine crews blowing their whistles at her when passing, sometimes leaning out of the cab at an alarming angle to give her a wave! Her much-concerned father sternly warned that if they were not careful they would fall out of their cabs one day! *(Date: 20 June 1985.)*

83
**Between Cole and Pitcombe
(Bridge No 121)**
(183 ST 671 334)

Ivatt 2-6-2T No 41242 prepares to
stop at Cole with an afternoon local
from Templecombe to Highbridge,
as it passes through the deep-sided
cutting south of the village.

Pitcombe Viaduct, just seen in
the distance, straddles the small
hamlet of Pitcombe, set in an attractive valley. *(Photo: Ivo Peters. Date:
19 May 1964.)*

Yet another example of backfilling.
A school's gang-mower breaks up
the monotonous view in the foreground, whilst the hills in the distance provide a familiar backdrop,
under which the track-bed survives
in good condition. *(Date: 18 June
1985.)*

84
Shepton Montague (1)
(183 ST 685 317)

Some fast running could be achieved through this glorious countryside. Seen here are the very grimy BR Class '4' 4-6-0 No 75027 and somewhat cleaner Bulleid Pacific No 34043 *Combe Martin* southbound with the 10.38 (SO) Manchester to Bournemouth (obviously devouring some dubious coal!)

To the north-east of this location the passengers would be able to see the beautiful mansion and grounds of Redlynch House set on a hill. *(Photo: Ivo Peters. Date: 7 July 1962.)*

The early summer's blossom adorns the trees and shrubs now envelop the banks of the track. Notice how many hedgerows have been removed in the 23 years between the photograph dates. Conversely see how the wood on the right hand side has grown! *(Date: 1 June 1985.)*

85
Shepton Montague (2)
(183 ST 687 316)

Class '3F' No 43216 in charge of
the 16.00 local from Highbridge to
Templecombe about to pass under
the twin portals of Bridge No 127 at
Shepton Montague.

Note how the lines diverge to go
under the bridge. Also the amount
excavated here during the line's
construction, most probably to
supply material for the long
embankments just north of here
(seen in previous photo). *(Photo:
Ivo Peters. Date: 2 September 1961.)*

The track-bed has been scavenged
for much-needed chippings, but
still provides a very solid surface.
The sides of the cutting have been
taken over by a mass of elder, but
the farm cottage in the background
is still visible from this position!
(Date: 1 June 1985.)

86
Shepton Montague (3)
(183 ST 687 315)

One of the last fertilizer specials from Avonmouth to Blandford to run over the S&D passes under the tall bridge (No 127) at Shepton Montague, hauled by S&D '7F' No 53806.

Soon after it became the Western Region's policy to re-route this traffic via Bristol, Bath Spa, Westbury, Salisbury, Southampton and Bournemouth; a journey of 135 miles instead of 65 over the S&D! This was but one example of how the line was deprived of its freight traffic. (*Photo: Ivo Peters. Date: 4 May 1963.*)

Elder and line trees encroach the cutting banks, but the bridge still stands out defiantly. Its tall and elegant structure provided ample clearance for trains, unlike most other bridges and tunnels on the system, which gave only minimum headroom. *(Date: 26 July 1984.)*

87

Near Wincanton

(183 ST 709 291)

On her final run over the Somerset & Dorset BR '9F' No 92214 rounds the bend just north of Wincanton with the 'Up Mail'. Soon the line would run straight and on a falling gradient towards Shepton Montague, enabling some speed to be built up.

It was on this long stretch that the line ran parallel to the minor road from Wincanton to Shepton Montague for over a mile. Ivo Peters was able to film a train from his car which was being driven by his son, issuing instructions to either speed up or slow down, as required to keep the train in frame!

This attractive setting was a favourite spot for lineside photographers. The sight of a heavy train coming round this bend against a backdrop of trees on the hill, perfectly summed up the line's many charms. *(Photo: Ivo Peters. Date: 20 June 1964.)*

The backdrop has not changed—the foreground has, although its heritage is left in no doubt. The fencing posts on either side are a tell-tale sign. The attractive twin-arched bridge from which this photograph was taken remains in good condition. *(Date: 3 June 1985.)*

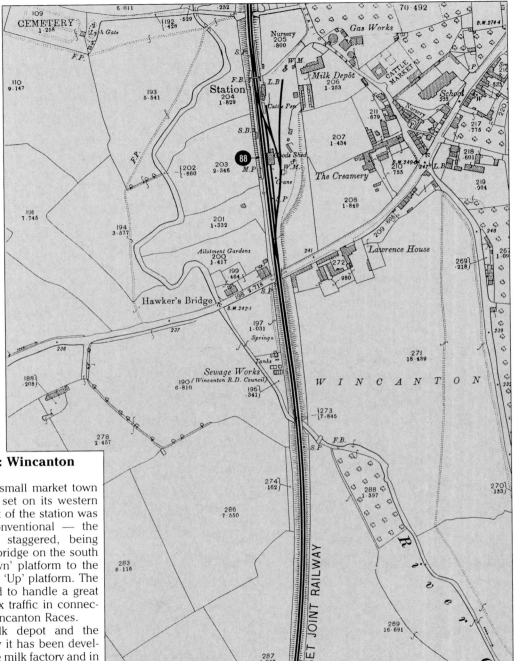

Map 21, 1903: Wincanton

Wincanton is a small market town with the station set on its western edge. The layout of the station was somewhat unconventional — the platforms were staggered, being linked by a footbridge on the south end of the 'Down' platform to the north end of the 'Up' platform. The goods yard used to handle a great deal of horsebox traffic in connection with the Wincanton Races.

Note the milk depot and the creamery. Today it has been developed into a large milk factory and in addition handles many associated dairy products. The 'Cow and Gate' siding used to handle considerable milk traffic to London, via Templecombe.

88
Wincanton Station
(183 ST 710 282)

SR Pacific No 34042, *Dorchester*, tears through Wincanton Station with a Bournemouth-bound express. Seen on the left of the 'Up' platform, behind the small shelter is the fourteen-lever signal box, complete with a block switch, controlling a fair sized layout. The small goods shed which housed a 30 cwt crane can just be seen on the left.

The staggered platforms overlapped for only 120 ft or so: access across was gained via the footbridge in the background. The 'Up' platform was 450 ft in length, the 'Down' platform 210 ft shorter! *(Photo: David Milton, Date: summer 1961.)*

This photograph was made possible with the kind help of an employee of the adjacent Unigate factory—who also happened to be an S&D fan! He used a fork lift truck to remove a large quantity of pallets (seen on the right) from the old 'Up' platform in order that I might obtain this shot. Whilst not exactly taken from the same position because of young trees growing immediately behind me, this still provides an interesting study. The last vestiges of the 'Up' platform can be clearly identified on the left. There are several old station lamp posts, one of which is seen on the left; some still have the remnants of the white shades hanging mournfully from their brackets, which have been used for airgun practice over the years.

One will notice the railway version of football hooligans invading the pitch in the form of new vehicles! The area between the platforms, now filled in, is used as a compound for their storage.

Note Wincanton Church tower on the right seen through the canopy of a new warehouse built on the site of the old goods shed. *(Date: 3 June 1985.)*

Chapter 8
Templecombe —Stourpaine and Durweston

Map 22, 1903: Templecombe

This map shows Templecombe in its railway heyday. Although a small village, its life was centred and built up around the railway. Most families had someone who either worked on the railway or had a connection with it in some way.

From 1870 S&D trains entered Templecombe Upper Station via No 2 Junction (seen just south of Hiscocks Lane.) 'Down' trains were able to enter straight into the station up the spur and into No 3 platform. They were then hauled back out by another engine attached at the rear, which was uncoupled when the train had passed No 2 Junction. The train then proceeded on its journey south passing Templecombe lower platform situated between a road overbridge and the main SR/LSWR main Waterloo to Exeter line.

'Up' trains were halted beyond No 2 Junction and the reverse procedure took place—a second engine would be coupled to the rear, and then haul the train up the spur to Templecombe Upper No 3 Platform. The 'Up' train then proceeded on its journey in the normal manner, having left its assistant standing in the platform!

The original Dorset Central Station building can be seen just south of the 50 ft turntable. The two-road engine shed, a wood and asbestos structure, was replaced with a red-brick building in 1950.

Templecombe was a scene of considerable activity, both for passenger and goods traffic. The upper and lower yards handled freight to and from far-flung areas.

Map 23, 1978: Templecombe

Standing on the platform at Templecombe today one cannot imagine the scene a mere twenty or thirty years ago. Trains coming and going, north and south, east and west. The Atlantic Coast Express—the premier SR train (run in as much as five separate portions on summer Saturdays) loaded with excited holidaymakers. The S&D going about its awkward business of getting trains in and out of No 3 platform—such variety—what a spectacle it all was.

Today Templecombe rises like a phoenix from the ashes, for its closure coincided with that of the S&D, on 6 March 1966. After lying dormant for seventeen years, it was opened once more for passenger traffic on 3 October 1983.

The double track section from Sherborne ends just west of the station at a crossover which provides a siding now shorter than the map shows, finishing level with the east end of the goods shed and occasionally being used by track maintenance vehicles. The main line, now reduced to a single track, runs through the station and on towards Salisbury and Waterloo.

Templecombe Shed survives today, together with a couple of other buildings from railway days. Plessey Marine have built an extensive factory on the site and have extended it to that shown on the map.

The overall layout depicted on the earlier map did not change drastically although Templecombe Upper Station was extensively rebuilt in 1938, the platforms extended to take fourteen coach trains and the track layout redesigned.

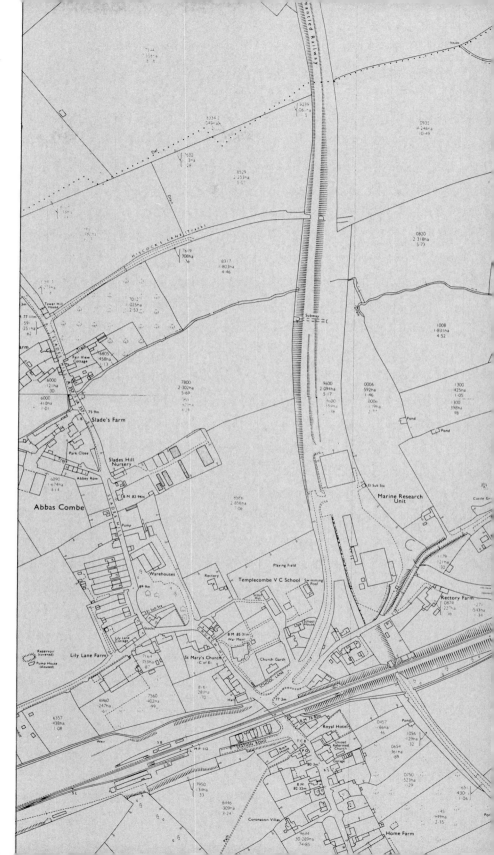

89
Templecombe No 2 Junction
(1) (183 ST 710 231)

Having called at the Southern Station, Templecombe Upper, S&D '7F' No 53807 and her train, the 07.43 (SO) Birmingham to Bournemouth, is hauled back down the spur to No 2 Junction before proceeding on her way to Bournemouth down the single line section to Blandford Forum seen in the foreground. The signal box which controlled No 2 Junction is seen in the background and to the right is a diminutive ex-SR 'G6' 0-6-0T No 30274 returning to shed after station pilot duty.

Two distinct signal designs seen either side of the engine are, on the left an SR/S&D type constructed from bolted rail sections and on the right the lattice L&SWR type. *(Photo: Ivo Peters. Date: 16 July 1955.)*

At first glance there is nothing to draw one's attention to the exact location, which looks rather like a tank training area! But lo and behold, a second look reveals two old signal bases which have been dug up and dumped by the side of the hedge—now look just under the '7F's right buffer!!

Insert So much useless scrap, the discarded base of a signal post. *(Date: 1 June 1985.)*

90
Templecombe No 2 Junction (2) (183 ST 709 231)

BR Class '9F' 2-10-0 No 92205 in charge of the 08.40 (SO) Bournemouth to Bradford train, sweeps up the sharp rise to No 2 Junction.

Templecombe Shed, usually a hive of activity, can be seen in the distance. It is at a lower level than the spur to Templecombe Upper pictured over the rear of the train, seen curving sharply to the right and around in front of the school building in the middle of the picture.

This photograph was taken from the signal box at No 2 Junction. *(Photo: Ivo Peters. Date: 13 August 1960.)*

The first problem in being able to take a facsimile photograph is to find out where you are! By the use of maps, tape, ruler and calculator the exact spot where No 2 box stood was found. The horizon reveals the church and school seen clearly in the original. The roof of Templecombe Shed can just be seen behind the factory units on the left.

The remains of the track-bed fall away sharply in the foreground to form a new car park. Extensive levelling has been undertaken here in the process of which the Templecombe Upper Spur has been removed almost completely. The far end is now made up as an access road from the village to the factory site. *(Date: 20 June 1985.)*

91
Templecombe Upper (SR)
spur (183 ST 709 226)

Ex-GWR 0-6-0 No 3206 departs with
an 'Up' local for Highbridge from
Templecombe Upper No 3 platform
with a three-coach train down the
spur towards No 2 Junction and
north.

The A357 road passed under two
bridges spanning the spur and platforms, seen in the background. The
extensive canopies of Templecombe Upper are clearly seen in
this interesting photograph. *(Photo:
E. Wilmshurst, via Ian Matthews.
Date: 16 June 1962.)*

Only the bridge parapet remains, the main A357 road clearly exposed, but it is the wooden building on the right which provides an instant clue as to the location. Note the retaining wall in front of the van which is visible in the original.

The back of the revitalized Templecombe Station's sign is seen above the bridge parapet, to the right of the wooden railings. *(Date: 16 June 1985.)*

92
Templecombe Upper (SR)
(183 ST 709 225)

SR 'S15' No 30843 with the 12.16 to Salisbury stands at Platform 2, whilst '4F' 0-6-0 No 44422 at Platform 3 is waiting on station pilot duty to haul the 12.23 to Bournemouth train back to No 2 Junction, where it will be uncoupled, allowing the train to proceed south on the single line section to Blandford and then on to Bournemouth.

Note the extensive structure of Templecombe Station, the buildings of which were rebuilt in the 'Art Deco' style around 1938.

The station is on a 1:150 gradient down towards Salisbury, increasing to 1:80 just east of the platforms. Occasionally trucks being shunted in the upper yard used to get away from their engine, to the alarm of the signalman who would see these breakaways going at quite a lick past the signal box windows and on down the 1:80 gradient, up the other side, back down again and so on in a reducing see-saw effect! If this happened during a busy period, it caused chaos. A shunting engine would then be sent down the gradient to collect the wayward trucks! *(Photo: via Ian Matthews. Date: 7 September 1963.)*

It is to the great credit of the Templecombe Station Working Committee and Somerset County Council that the station is enjoying a new lease of life today. It reopened for a three-year trial period on 3 October 1983, an initial annual target being set by BR of £31,000. This was achieved in the first six months and currently the takings are in the region of £1,500 per week. No 3 platform has been fenced off, but the old S&D track-bed is still visible, despite becoming overgrown.

The platform has been reconstructed and can cope easily with the eight-coach sets predominantly using the line. It is somewhat shorter than before, the platform finishing just to the west of the road bridge seen in both photographs. The signal box is used as a ticket office and waiting room combined and also retains a sixteen-lever electro-mechanical frame (at one time there were sixty levers in this box!)

Class '50' No 50011, *Centurion*, tears past Templecombe platform with the 09.38 Exeter St David's to Waterloo train.

Right and below left Templecombe Station and signal box and the carefully tended sixteen-lever frame—clearly maintained in the best railway traditions. *(Date: 20 June 1985.)*

93
Templecombe Shed
(183 ST 710 228)

A splendid photograph taken of Templecombe Shed, as rebuilt in 1950, which provides an excellent indication of the variety of motive power to be seen on the line. On the left is a station pilot and upper yard shunter in the form of SR Class 'Z' 0-8-0 No 30954: just to the right of '3F' No 43216 is an SR Class 'G6' 0-6-0T. The others include '2P' No 40568 seen in the foreground, and behind that a BR Class '5' 4-6-0, together with two '3F's and a '4F' at the rear. Further '4F's are visible in the shed and also on the spur which once led to the Salisbury and Yeovil line.

The line in the foreground passed under the bridge to Templecombe Lower platform and then on south to Bournemouth. *(Photo: W. Vaughan Jenkins, via R. Atthill. Date: winter 1958.)*

The old engine shed has survived and forms part of an extensive factory complex. The bridge over the line to Bournemouth can just be seen behind the helicopter (with the number '61' on its nose, background right). Two small railway buildings survive to the rear of the shed. *(Date: 1 June 1985.)*

94
Templecombe Shed
(183 ST 710 227)

Going? Templecombe Shed plays host to a variety of locomotives, including in the foreground '2P' 4-4-0 No 40537 with a sister engine up front. The now preserved '4F' No 44422 is seen adjacent to the original Dorset Central Station buildings. BR Class '5MT' No 73047 is seen just beyond the turntable, whilst S&D Class '7F' 2-8-0 No 53804 is pictured in the background.

The running line to Bournemouth is in the foreground. Just seen on the far left is the spur to Templecombe Upper.

This photograph was taken from Bridge 152 in Combe Throop Lane. *(Photo: R. C. Riley. Date: 7 July 1959.)*

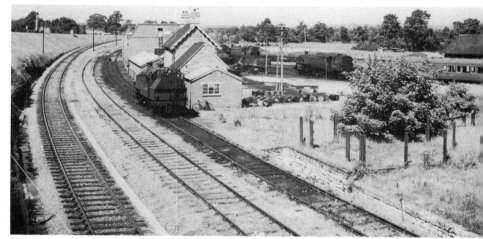

Going . . . Templecombe Shed seen here in its latter days and only a shadow of its former self. 2-6-2T and 2-6-4T tank engines predominate. A solitary BR Class '4' can be seen behind the engine shed. The original Dorset Central Station buildings are seen in the middle of the photograph. The running line to Bournemouth is in the foreground. Just seen on the far left is the spur to Templecombe Upper. *(Photo: David Milton. Date: summer 1965.)*

Now gone Invaders from outer space so far as steam locomotives are concerned. A Westland Wessex HAS 3, *XS149*, used for static testing purposes, stands on the old track-bed. The extensive factory area can be observed from this photograph. The Templecombe Shed still stands out defiantly—'a rose amongst thorns'. Also of note are the other two surviving railway buildings seen between the helicopter and engine shed. *(Date: 20 June 1985.)*

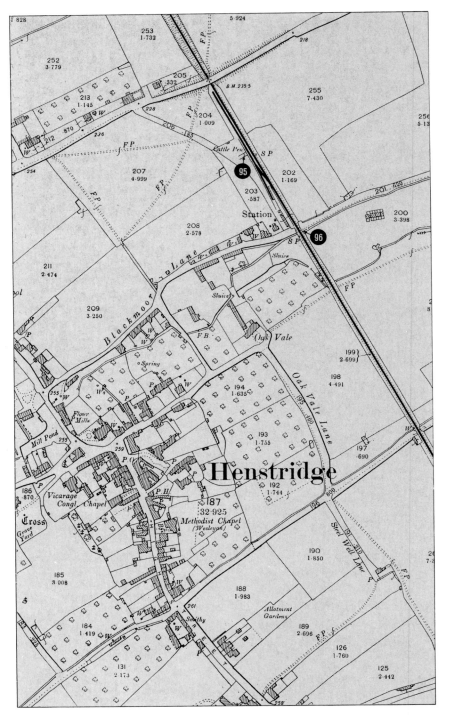

Map 24, 1903: Henstridge

Two miles from Templecombe No 2 Junction on the single track section to Blandford Forum Henstridge Station is passed.

Henstridge was the smallest station on the S&D. The buildings were of wooden structure but contained such facilities as ladies' and gentlemen's waiting rooms, booking office and urinal! There was a small goods yard controlled by a ground frame. It provided both a milk dock and cattle pen. Today the platform survives, together with the base of the cattle pen. The site is now used as a scrap yard.

95
Henstridge Station (1)
(183 ST 726 202)

BR Class '5' 4-6-0 No 73022 passes Henstridge Station with a Southern Wanderers enthusiasts' special.

Henstridge, on a single line section, was not a block post and had no passing loop. A ground frame controlled the small siding seen in the foreground. This photograph was taken from the cattle loading dock. *(Photo: Ivo Peters. Date: 28 March 1965.)*

Poor Henstridge! The platform is still just visible, but now overgrown with scrub and small trees. The station goods yard area is now an untidy scrap yard. Various tote bins, skips and pallets litter the site. *(Date: 17 April 1985.)*

96
Henstridge Station (2)
(183 ST 726 201)

The neat and tidy appearance of this small station can be seen to good effect. Nice touches like the bicycle propped against the station building go to make a tranquil scene. Bridge No 159 seen here to the north carries the busy A30 trunk road.

Note the small goods yard with loading gauge, cattle pen and two coal trucks. In the foreground is the level crossing gate post. *(Photo: R. C. Riley. Date: 4 July 1961.)*

The crossing gate remains firmly shut—the post now overgrown with ivy. The platform and track-bed are covered by a mass of small trees and scrub. The embankment carrying the A30 main road can just be seen through a gap in the trees. The track-bed to the south of the level crossing, however, remains in reasonable condition, although one or two old cars have been dumped on the section. *(Date: 3 June 1985.)*

97
Stalbridge (183 ST 739 181)

This was the first block post south of Templecombe and had a crossing loop running through the station —the 'Up' line having the straight run through. The station buildings of typical Dorset Central design, were on the 'Up' side. A signal box just out of view on the left had eighteen levers and controlled the small goods yard to the north of the station and also the level crossing. Note the hand-operated crane in the yard. *(Photo: R. C. Riley. Date: 4 July 1961.)*

Which scene do you prefer? Believe it or not, this scene marks the location of Stalbridge Station. The whole area has been built over by a steel stockholder. Not one artefact could I find to act as a link with the past, except an oil painting dated 1979 hanging in the reception area by H. Ball, a local artist, depicting '2P' No 40700 piloting a Stanier 'Black Five' through Stalbridge Station on a 'Down' 'Pines Express' and a slight bump in the road, which was the position of the level crossing.

Between Templecombe and Stalbridge, there were no fewer than six manned level crossings where most of the keepers' cottages and some original gates survive: Common Lane, Park Lane, Plott Lane, Marsh Lane, South Mead and Drews Lane. The line immediately south of Stalbridge Station has been extensively developed into an industrial site. *(Date: 3 June 1985.)*

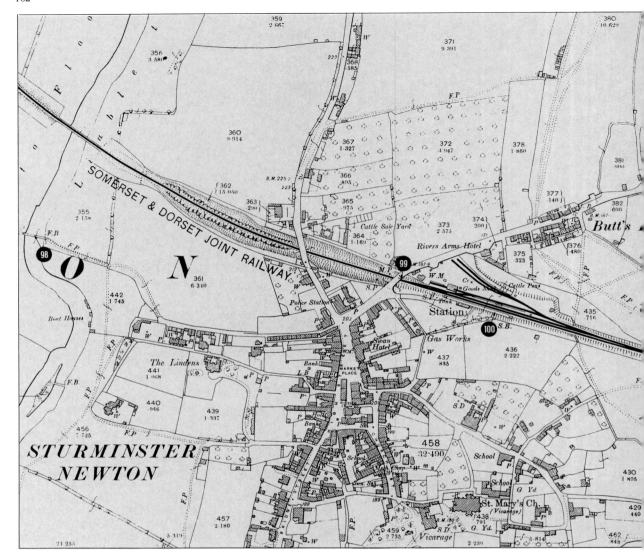

Map 25, 1902: Sturminster Newton

Southbound trains entering Sturminster Newton crossed the River Stour and, over the course of the next nine miles, would do so again on a further three occasions.

The attractive market town of Sturminster generated a fair amount of cattle and milk traffic and ample handling facilities were provided for such. The goods shed was of red-brick construction and the station buildings were of Dorset Central design. The platforms, like Wincanton, were staggered, but only slightly by comparison. The 'Up' platform had a dip in it to provide a crossing facility to the 'Down' side, since no footbridge was provided.

Today a car park covers the station site. There are few reminders of the area's past employment.

98
Sturminster Newton bridge over the River Stour
(194 ST 783 143)

This was the first of the four flirtations that southbound trains had with the River Stour over the ensuing nine miles. However, SR Pacific 34041, *Wilton*, on the 11.40 (SO) Bournemouth to Derby train here crosses the Stour for the last time on her journey northwards.

This photograph conjures up thoughts of halcyon summer days spent lazing by the river with splendid picnics, watching the trains rumble back and forth over the bridge! The truth is more likely to be that one treads in a cowpat, the children get bitten by mosquitos, the wife finds a fly has dropped in her tea, granny gets stung by a wasp found in her jam sandwich, whilst grandpa loses his false teeth and gets sunburnt on his bald pate! *(Photo: Ivo Peters. Date: 2 August 1959.)*

They say a picture is worth a thousand words, so here is the same scene today! *(Date: 20 June 1985.)*

Would Horatius have managed to save this bridge? The derelict edifice wears its age and misfortune with quiet dignity, above the water meadows, in the early calm of a peaceful May morning. *(Date: May 1985.)*

99
Sturminster Newton (1) (194 ST 788 142)

Located half way between the sixteen mile Temple-combe to Blandford Forum single line section, the attractive market town of Sturminster Newton was reached. The station had a crossing loop with the 'Up' road being given the straight run through, in line with S&D practice.

'I think I can, I think I can', must have been '4F' 0-6-0 No 44422's song this day. She has been given the eight-coach train of the 14.45 (SO) Bournemouth to Bristol, seen here setting off from Sturminster Newton. Hopefully she would have adequate assistance waiting for her at Evercreech Junction for the climb over the Mendips.

Note Ivo Peters' Bentley waiting in the station yard. How many 'buffs' will recognize the Seddon lorry? Hambledon Hill, upon which there is a neolithic camp, can be seen in the distance. *(Photo: Ivo Peters. Date: 16 July 1960.)*

Hambledon Hill provides the link, otherwise it would take a very keen eye to spot any other similarity. Note the section of roof just showing on the left-hand side as being that in the original. The whole area has been given over to a car park, the land graded accordingly, providing access to a supermarket and the adjacent businesses, including an agricultural merchant and a carpet warehouse built on the site of the old goods yard and shed. *(Date: 20 June 1985.)*

100
Sturminster Newton (2)
(194 ST 789 141)

A good view of the 'Up' platform looking north and under the B3091 road bridge. Note the gas light on the left of the platform and the neat goods shed opposite.

The peculiar dip in the 'Up' platform, providing access across the track to the 'Down' side, is seen just this side of the schoolgirl. I wonder how many people absentmindedly stepped out of a train on a dark night into this abyss! *(Photo: David Milton. Date: summer 1961.)*

The changes here are dramatic, but the two buildings on the right provide continuity, as does the tree on the far left on the horizon.

The B3091 road bridge (S&D No 173) has been demolished and the road levelled. The land between Bridges 173 and 172 has been partially infilled. On the north side of Bridge 172, which carries the B3092, the land has been infilled almost back to the bridge over the Stour. *(Date: 17 April 1985.)*

101
Shillingstone (194 ST 825 117)

Seen here is Shillingstone Station located on the north-east side of the village and adjacent to the River Stour. The building on the 'Up' side had a large and ornate awning supposedly in honour of King Edward VII who used the station for his visits to nearby Iwerne Minster House.

The station had a small goods yard on the 'Up' side and a sixteen-lever wooden signal box in front of which, this fine study of Shillingstone was taken. *(Photo: David Milton. Date: summer 1961.)*

A late evening study of the same view today. It is remarkable how relatively unchanged the station is —albeit the track-bed is overgrown with weeds. A shed has been built on the track-bed at the southern end of the platforms. The nameboard posts survive on the 'Down' platform but are obscured by undergrowth.

The colour of the awning is chocolate and cream—much to the chagrin of S&D enthusiasts, one would suspect! The building itself is used as a workshop. Note how the trees have grown since the original photograph was taken.

The goods yard has been developed into a small industrial estate, but the shed used for animal feed, which was part of the latter day layout, survives. *(Date: 3 June 1985.)*

102
Cliff Bridge (No 183)
(194 ST 844 102)

Approximately two miles south of Shillingstone Station, the line passed under Cliff Bridge through a deep cutting. The line courted the River Stour all the way to Blandford, passing through magnificent country; the chalk downs and Hod Hill to the east provided interesting features, together with the abundantly wooded hills of Blandford Forest on the south-western side of the line.

S&D Class '7F' 2-8-0 No 53810 heading north up the long straight from Stourpaine, is about to pass under Cliff Bridge with the 11.12 (SO) Bournemouth to Sheffield train. *(Photo: Ivo Peters. Date: 22 July 1961.)*

The cutting has proved a convenient dumping ground for spoil removed from the recently completed Blandford by-pass. The distant views to the attractive village of Stourpaine with the chalk downs as a backdrop give an idea of the beautiful countryside found beyond this sad scene. *(Date: 3 June 1985.)*

103
Stourpaine and Durweston Halt (194 ST 860 091)

This station was another latecomer to the S&D scene, but was closed after only 28 years of operation. Opened on 9 July 1928 between the two villages of Stourpaine and Durweston, adjacent to the River Stour, it was built to the typical SR style in pre-fabricated concrete. Its shelter was built at a later date and stood over the embankment on precarious looking concrete stilts!

Half a mile to the north of the station there was a crossing loop, controlled by a small signal box, which broke up the 5½-mile block section from Shillingstone to Blandford. Subsequently this was removed and the signal box closed on 18 December 1951. *(Photo: Lens of Sutton. Date: 9 July 1928.)*

Obscured by trees in the summer, a direct facsimile shot is impossible, but by walking up the embankment to the bridge just south of the platform, this view is obtained. The halt is in good condition, despite superficial vandalism. *(Date: 20 June 1985.)*

Near Prestleigh
(183 ST 633 408)

The LCGB 'Farewell Special', one of the last trains to traverse the S&D, hauled by 'West Country' Class No 34006 *Bude* and 'Battle of Britain' Class No 34057 *Biggin Hill*, immaculately prepared for the occasion, tackles with consummate ease the climb towards Cannard's Grave after crossing Prestleigh Viaduct, with its nine-coach train. *(Photo: Mrs Angela O'Shea. Date: 5 March 1966.)*

Late autumn sunshine highlights the hill that once provided the backdrop to the S&D. The last remaining section of the S&D's embankment adjacent to Prestleigh Viaduct is clearly visible in the sunlight to the right of the photograph. It was on this section that one of the final scenes of the BBC's film 'Return to Evercreech Junction' was shot.

The greater proportion of the line's formation has been wiped off the face of the earth at this location and the land put back to agricultural use. The two pylons on the horizon provide a good reference point but the one in the foreground was obscured by steam in the 1966 photograph. *(Date: 15 November 1985.)*

Evercreech Junction (North)
(183 ST 636 371)

Fireman Keith Conibear gets ready to hand the single-line token from West Pennard to the signalman at Evercreech Junction North Box, as '3F' 0-6-0 No 43436 with the 14.20 ex-Highbridge prepares to leave the 'branch' before running down to Evercreech Junction Station on the main line.

The weighbridge hut, shunters' cabin and lamp room can be seen on the right of the photograph, behind which was the 56ft turntable located in the centre of the 'V' formed by the divergence of the main line and the branch. *(Photo: R. C. Riley (2026). Date: 6 July 1959.)*

The whole area has been returned to pasture land. The only surviving railway artefact adjacent to 'North Box' is the guards' cabin and mess room seen in the middle distance. The solitary tree provided me with the only tangible reference point visible in the 1959 photograph.

Just seen in the distance between the tree and the cabin is Prestleigh Viaduct, which is some 2¼ miles away, as the crow flies.

The audience was kindly herded and positioned by Mike Arlett. Before his timely intervention they refused to co-operate and insisted on both licking my leg and nudging my rear whilst I was trying to photograph this location! *(Date: 2 November 1985.)*

Wyke Champflower
(Bridge 115) (183 ST 661 343)

'4MT' 2-6-4T No 80013 passes under the bridge at Wyke Champflower with a 'Down' local. It will soon round Cole Curve upon which there was a permanent 45mph speed restriction. *(Photo: R. C. Riley (8791). Date: September 1965.)*

The bridge has been backfilled on the north side, but provides good shelter for the cattle that now graze on this section of line.

Further north no trace of the railway can be found at Bruton Road Crossing except for new sections of fencing placed in the gaps left in the hedge. Lamyatt crossing keeper's cottage is now a private dwelling and the line formation northwards in the direction of Evercreech Junction is well defined.

Autumn colours highlight the few remaining trees in the area. Considerable thinning, both natural and by man, has befallen the trees in the background. *(Date: 18 November 1985.)*

Cole Viaduct (183 ST 668 337)

2-6-4T No 80059 heads north with the 15.40 'Up Mail' and passes over Cole Viaduct on a beautiful summer's evening. The cattle seem quite undisturbed and wander down to the River Brue to quench their thirst. *(Photo: Mrs Angela O'Shea. Date: 26 June 1965.)*

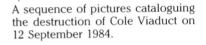

A sequence of pictures cataloguing the destruction of Cole Viaduct on 12 September 1984.

The last vestiges of an autumn afternoon's sun catch the embankment of the viaduct which once carried the S&D over the River Brue and a farm track.

However, the contractors have made a good job of tidying up the area, causing little or no damage to the surrounding environment. Only a small portion of the viaduct piers remain and help to keep the River Brue from eroding the bank at that point. *(Date: 15 November 1985.)*

Chapter 9
Blandford Forum— Bournemouth

Map 26, 1929: Blandford Forum

Upon entering Blandford Station double track was regained, remaining so for the next eight miles to Corfe Mullen.

The station was of Dorset Central design and both the largest and most important on the S&D. The main buildings, faced with a large canopy, were on the 'Up' platform. The 'Down' platform was modest by comparison and was overshadowed by a tall signal box, which was struck by lightning and gutted by fire in 1906. The station also had a goods shed and in addition boasted a subway.

The remains of the 'Old Military Siding' can be seen. This once led to the nearby army camp, but became disused in 1921. The River Stour was crossed again for the last time just to the south of the town. The map is full of interesting detail and is cartographically delightful!

Today the station site has been built upon, only the pedestrian footbridge just north of the station survives.

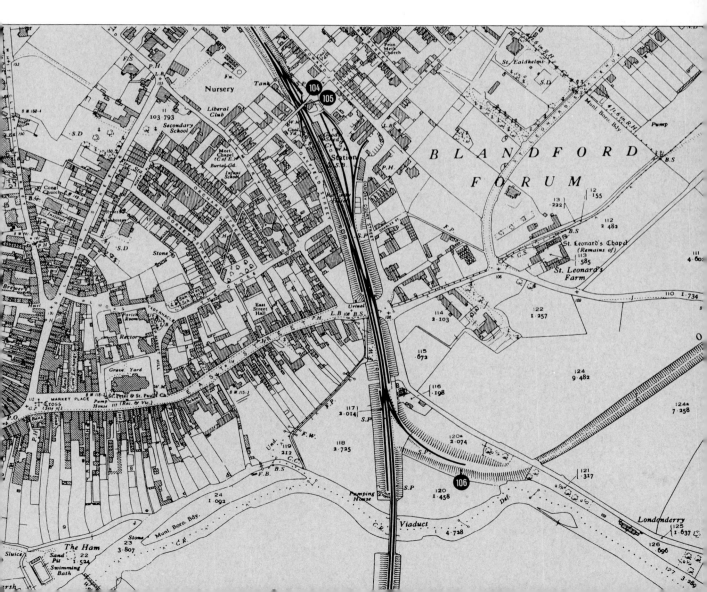

104
Blandford Forum
(194 ST 888 067)

BR Class '5' 4-6-0 No 73047 drifts down the 1:80 gradient under the Salisbury road bridge at Blandford Forum with an excursion from Bristol to Bournemouth and has just regained double track before passing through the station. Note the tall 'Up' starting signal, which could be clearly seen from the other side of the footbridge and to the south of the station. Note the old loading dock on the right, served by a short siding. *(Photo: Ivo Peters. Date: 5 August 1963.)*

The base of the old water tank is still visible on the left, as is the building behind the trees. The track-bed has been made into a linear park, along which a good walk to the northern outskirts of the town is provided.

Left and below left The footbridge (Bridge No 194) survives still with one steam/smoke deflector in its middle and directly underneath, a short piece of track with a rail sectioned buffer provides a tentative link with the past. *(Date: 23 May 1985.)*

105
Blandford Forum
(194 ST 888 067)

A fine view of Blandford Forum station clearly showing the extensive layout of the largest station on the S&D system. The slightly shorter 'Down' platform makes way for the goods shed seen on the left. The tall signal box located just beyond commands a good view north and south. The jib of the seven-ton crane in the goods yard is just poking above the shed.

Note that no footbridge was built here—the station was provided with a subway instead. *(Photo: David Milton. Date: summer 1961.)*

Believe me—this was Blandford Station! The whole site is now dominated by a variety of modern housing. The start of the linear park is seen marked by a gate at the bottom of the photograph. The goods yard area has been converted into a car park.

Two tangible links with the past can just be seen in this photograph, the tree on the horizon to the left of the picture, and the chimneys of a hotel over the roof of the house in the foreground. *(Date: 22 May 1985.)*

106
Blandford Forum (Bridge No 198) (194/195 ST 890 062)

The last southbound crossing of the Stour was made just after leaving Blandford Station. Seen here is BR '9F' 2-10-0 No 92206 crossing the lattice girder bridge with the 08.16 (SO) Bournemouth West to Liverpool Lime Street. The bridge was very similar in design to the one at Sturminster Newton. *(Photo: Ivo Peters. Date: 16 July 1960.)*

The last vestiges of the bridge grimly cling on to a useless existence. The arches on the southern bank have been removed, together with the embankments, for use in constructing the Blandford by-pass. The old line formation is now just a chalk scar extending into the distance.

This photograph was taken on a hazy day in poor lighting conditions near to but not in exactly the same position as the original shot and provides a stark contrast to the sunny July day in 1960. *(Date: 22 May 1985.)*

107
Charlton Marshall Halt
(195 ST 898 040)

This section of track provided an opportunity for some fast running, having an official speed limit of 70 mph, which was often exceeded if 'everything was right'! The halt was short lived, like Stourpaine and Durweston, opening only four days previously on 5 July 1928, it closed on the same date—17 September 1956.

This classic study shows BR Class '4' 4-6-0 No 75071 dipping under the bridge at 1:100 to pass Charlton Marshall Halt with the 09.05 (SO) Bristol to Bournemouth. The switchback effect of the line from Blandford is seen to excellent advantage in this photograph. *(Photo: Ivo Peters. Date: 16 July 1960.)*

I had the good fortune to be accompanied by Peter Smith on my foray to the halt to take this photograph. So we got busy in this fly-infested cutting, pruning back some branches and brambles to get this study of the bridge (S&D No 203). The platforms remain in good shape, but are somewhat overgrown. The steps to both the 'Up' and 'Down' platforms are used by walkers to gain access to the old track. Peter informed me that this halt was the devil to find when driving a train on a dark night, because of the poor lighting on the platforms! *(Date: 23 May 1985.)*

108
Spetisbury Halt
(195 ST 908 029)

No suitable photograph availed itself of Spetisbury in its heyday.
These photographs show the remaining vestiges of this halt which
closed in September 1956, along
with its two northerly neighbours.
Below The steps to the 'Up' platform
from the minor road under Bridge
215.
Right Peter Smith surveys the scene,
standing on Spetisbury's 'Up' platform.
Below right View of Spetisbury Halt
looking north.
(Date: 4 June 1985.)

109
Bailey Gate Station
(195 SY 949 995)

Bailey Gate Station was of basic Dorset Central design. The 'Down' platform was provided with a brick station building and a wooden porters' cabin, seen on the extreme left. The 'Up' platform had a small wooden shelter. The squat signal box of 24 levers and a block switch controlled a fair-sized layout. The major feature in the background is the United Dairies milk processing factory (formerly Carters & Dorset Modern Dairies). This provided the line with considerable milk traffic to London via Wimborne until 1933, when it was re-routed through Templecombe. Stored in the background are barrels of whey!

'Down' expresses used to roar through this station, having picked up good speed on the falling 1:100 gradient on a gently curving stretch of line. Similarly, 'Up' trains, following a fast descent of Corfe Mullen bank were able to achieve a good speed past here. *(Photo: David Milton. Date: summer 1961.)*

Taken on a dull and overcast evening, Bailey Gate's platforms are still quite distinct. This picture taken from the road bridge (S&D No 220) graphically shows how the fortunes have changed for the milk factory. Although partly retained, the site is used as small industrial units. Note the goods yard stripped of all its vestiges, save an old boat stored in the small bay. *(Date: 23 May 1985.)*

110
Bailey Gate Crossing
(195 SY 969 986)

A Post Office telephone engineer cleans himself up whilst parked next to the tall signal box controlling the crossing on the A31 Dorchester to Wimborne road.

It was a signal and telegraph engineer who bore witness to the occasion when an unfortunate Templecombe driver working the 06.55 Bath to Bournemouth, smashed through the crossing gates, reducing them to matchwood. A passing motorist, forced to stop whilst the debris was cleared, asked the engineer as to the cause. The answer was given in true 'Old Bill' style—'Termites!' *(Photo: David Milton. Date: spring 1961.)*

The empty road is an illusion! I did not risk trying to take this photograph from the exact position of the original as I had no wish to play ducks and drakes with articulated lorries and continental juggernauts. I took this shot from the relative safety of the verge on this busy main road. The base of the old signal box is seen—the keeper's cottage being in better condition today than it was in the '60s. A nanny goat was grazing in front of it on the old track bed—a reminder of when a driver found a goat on the line and took it back home with him in the cab of his locomotive! *(Date: 4 June 1985.)*

111

Corfe Mullen Junction and Crossing (195 SY 978 983)

The original Dorset Central Line ran east from Corfe Mullen to join, via a trailing junction, the L&SWR at Wimborne, which meant S&D trains had to reverse before proceeding to Bournemouth. However, the S&D built a new line in 1884/5. Three miles long from Corfe Mullen to Broadstone it joined the L&SWR there. In 1933 the old route to Wimborne was truncated, but a mile of the track was retained to serve Carter's Siding.

BR Class '9F' No 92204 with the 08.40 (SO) Bournemouth to Bradford train approaches Corfe Mullen at the end of the three-mile section from Broadstone, a good run down the 1:80 falling gradient, having enabled some speed to be gained.

Legend has it that Donald Beale achieved an estimated 80 mph on this section, driving a Bulleid Pacific on the 'Up' 'Pines'. He was accompanied at the time by Inspector Jack Hookey who was being thrown about in the cab by the oscillations of the locomotive as it rounded the curve past the signal box, prompting the alarmed inspector to yell above the din, 'I think you're going plenty fast enough, Donald'. 'You'll be alright!' came the reply—and on blasted the Pacific! It was only after the BR Standard locomotives, which were fitted with speedometers, entered service that true speeds were accurately gauged! *(Photo: Ivo Peters. Date: 16 July 1960.)*

Due to the growth of elder trees, the exact facsimile was not possible to take. However, I felt that this junction was of significance in the S&D's history and therefore I took this shot from the middle of the B3074 road bridge. The track-bed is kept well grazed by a large rabbit population. The cutting in which Corfe Mullen Halt once stood has now been filled in.

Bottom left Corfe Mullen crossing showing the last piece of S&D track. This image was taken from the site of the signal box that used to control the crossing. *(Date: 4 June 1985.)*

Map 27, 1924/1928
Broadstone Junction

The S&D's own system ended here, joining the SR/L&SWR's Wimborne to Hamworthy Junction line. The single S&D section from Corfe Mullen crossed over the L&SWR to enter the eastern platforms, regaining double track in the process.

The station buildings, which were rather squat and dominated by tall chimneys, seemed to be out of proportion to the ample platform space provided for this once busy interchange station. The signal box, a substantial brick structure, housed a 33-lever frame pre-war. The covered footbridge bestrode the platforms like a Colossus, rather dominating the station.

The 1932 version of this map shows the 'Up' L&SWR/SR line cut south of the station becoming no more than a carriage siding, the track being singled to Hamworthy. The Junction, once on the L&SWR Dorchester-Waterloo main route via Wimborne and Brockenhurst, lost most of its importance once the causeway was built over Holes Bay, linking Hamworthy and Poole in 1893.

Today nothing remains of the station except the old station master's house and railwaymen's cottages. A new housing development is under construction.

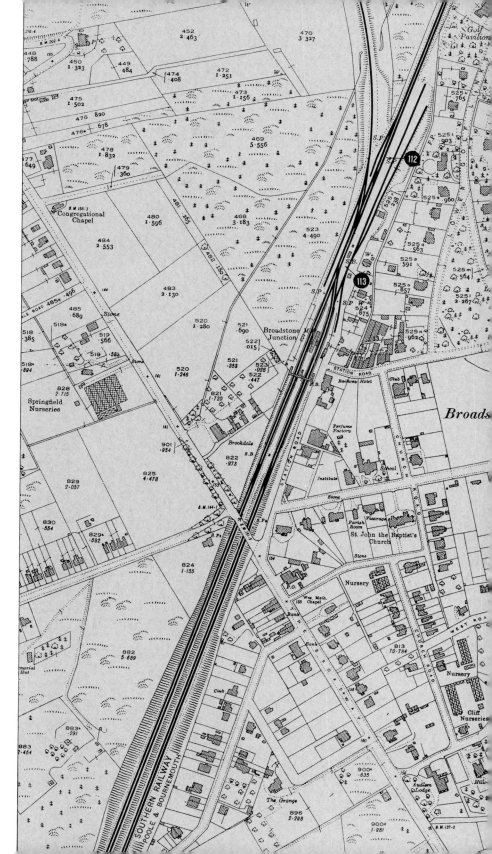

112
Broadstone Junction
(195 SY 005 963)

This photograph, taken from an L&SWR signal post, shows BR '9F' No 92203 snaking through Broadstone Station with the 09.55 (SO) Bournemouth to Leeds to take the single line section to Corfe Mullen, which was the point at which the S&D's own track was gained: 63¾ miles to Bath lay ahead. The track in the foreground is the old L&SWR line from Brockenhurst passing straight through the station and into the distance towards Hamworthy Junction. Broadstone's large footbridge can be seen above the train.

Broadstone marked the point where S&D trains traversed SR track for the final eight miles to Bournemouth West. (Photo: Ivo Peters. Date: 16 July 1960.)

To highlight the problems of facsimile work, I had to be elevated by a mechanical loader to some 21 ft or more, standing precariously on a small wooden pallet, much to the amazement of my companion that day, Peter Smith. Looking down at him from my perch, his incredulous expression was a sight to behold!

The weather was far from ideal, being hazy and thundery, the visibility poor. However this is Broadstone Junction today. At first glance there is not much similarity save the trees on the right horizon. On the left side the end of a roof of an old railway cottage can just be seen.

The road in the foreground provides access to the nearby newly-built club house of the golf club, long since established. The old S&D single track disappears to the right and continues for 200 yards before vanishing. The occasional signal wire pulley can be seen still at the side of the line formation.

This area will soon be a mass of new houses and bungalows, but fortunately some vestiges have been saved—the station building was removed and is to be re-erected at Medstead and Four Marks on the 'Watercress Line'. *(Date: 4 June 1985.)*

113

Broadstone (195 SY 005 962)

With driver Bert Brewer in charge, SR Pacific No 34041, *Wilton*, tackles the point work at Broadstone Station and swings towards the single line section to Corfe Mullen with the 09.25 (SO) Bournemouth to Manchester. Note the squat station building and to its rear the Broadstone Hotel. *(Photo: Ivo Peters. Date: 16 July 1960.)*

The only recognizable feature today is the Broadstone Hotel, seen on the left. A new housing development will cover the site completely. *(Date: 4 June 1985.)*

Map 28, 1936: Holes Bay Junction and Poole

The S&D trains drawing near to Poole merged with the Southern Weymouth-Waterloo main line at Holes Bay Junction.

This map shows Poole's marshalling yards, which are similar in layout today though some sidings have been shortened. The goods shed and associated sidings were removed to make way for a car park. Poole Station, built on a sharp curve, is seen at the bottom of the map. All S&D trains had to stop here.

There has been considerable land reclamation since publication of this map and extensive industrial development in the area, especially at Holes Bay. Factories and industrial units now cover the site of the old railway line from Broadstone.

Poole is still a busy modern station. Until their closure a year or two ago the freight yards enjoyed considerable traffic which included a Blue Circle Cement terminal, but the sidings are still used to berth inter-regional passenger trains to the Bournemouth area, which normally start or terminate at Poole.

114
Holes Bay Junction
(195 SY 011 919)

S&D Class '7F' No 53808 with the 07.43 (SO) Birmingham to Bournemouth train joins the Southern main line from Weymouth to Waterloo at Holes Bay, which skirted round the bay on a causeway, part of which is just visible on the left. *(Photo: Ivo Peters. Date: 7 August 1954.)*

Again, the dramatic changes are evident in this shot. It was taken on a filthy wet afternoon with very bad lighting conditions, from the shelter of an umbrella kindly held by the ever-tolerant Peter Smith, acting as guide for the day!
    The extent of industrial development can be judged from this photograph. Land reclamation for this purpose in the area has been extensive, the junction long since removed. However, close examination will reveal the odd 1930s' house as being the same! *(Date: 4 June 1985.)*

Map 29, 1933: Branksome Junction

Better known as Branksome Triangle for obvious reasons, Branksome was at a point where S&D trains entered Bournemouth West by branching right at Branksome Station and then past Branksome Shed, which is seen at the southeast section of the triangle. The shed was built of asbestos and corrugated iron around a timber frame and had two roads. Bourne-

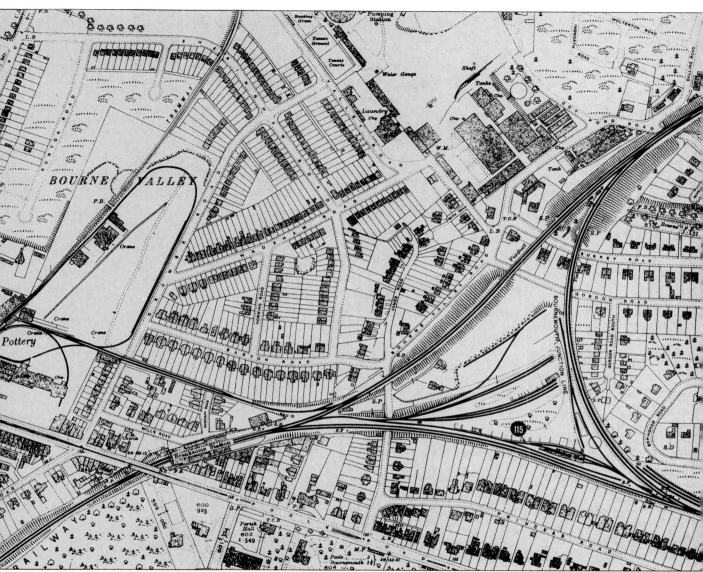

mouth Central and London-bound trains carried straight on heading north-east.

The notorious Bournemouth West curve is seen clearly where trains of eight coaches or more, if halted by signals before entering Bournemouth West, often had extreme difficulty in restarting. This was particularly true when being hauled by a slippery-footed Bulleid Pacific! If this happened either an engine was despatched from the nearby shed to assist the train in trouble, or somebody would lend a hand by throwing a shovel or two of sand, strategically placed under the slipping wheels of the locomotive.

Branksome Shed closed on 1 January 1963 and was demolished in 1965. The track on Bournemouth West curve was lifted around 1968, being disused from 1 November 1965. The sidings in the goods yard were removed on 29 November 1970.

Trains now using the carriage sidings and cleaning plant on the old Bournemouth West section have to reverse in one direction if travelling to or from Bournemouth Central, halting by Branksome Station before doing so.

115
Branksome Shed
(195 SY 062 919)

This pre-war study of the small Branksome shed taken from the west end shows '4F' 0-6-0 No 3898 standing in No 2 shed road. The small enginemen's mess room is seen directly underneath the water tank. On the right are the running lines to Bournemouth West Station, approximately 1¼ miles to the east. The shed closed on 1 January 1963. *(Photo: R. C. Riley. Date: 2 July 1938.)*

On 23 May 1985 I was privileged to have the company of both Donald Beale and Peter Smith, two ex-Branksome men, who were revisiting the site for the first time since they left railway employ. For a while I left them to wander around the site wrapped up in their memories and later photographed them together against once familiar backdrops, including the now defunct viaduct of the Bournemouth West curve.

I paid another visit with Peter Smith on 4 June: again he had to hold an umbrella in the pouring rain whilst I took this photograph of the site. Note the carriages on the right! The same trees seen in the 1938 photograph can be picked out in the background. *(Date: 4 June 1985.)*

Branksome Tales

I listened with tears of laughter pouring down my cheeks to some of Peter's anecdotes emanating from the enginemen's mess room at Branksome. A couple I must share . . .

One summer Sunday morning, whilst standing at the trackside adjacent to Bournemouth West Junction signal box, awaiting the arrival of a Bulleid 'Pacific' from Bournemouth Central shed with which to work the 09.45 to Bristol, Bert Brewer and Peter Smith were hailed by the box's harrassed occupant, known to local railwaymen as 'Yorkie'.

'What a shift I'm having,' he yelled down in despairing tones. 'There's flippin' trains everywhere this morning—I haven't stopped since I came on duty!' Whereupon Bert, one of the many characters that the S&D produced, and who sometimes did not get things *quite* right, shouted back, 'You'm like the Scarlet Pimple then, mate—you sees 'em here, you sees 'em there, you sees the buggers everywhere!'

The mess room was also the scene of many a heated political discussion. Two well-known protagonists used to argue the point, one remaining quite calm and carrying on eating his sandwiches, whilst the other, getting quite irate and perched on the edge of his seat, face to face with his opponent would usually end up after a few exchanges of 'Yes t'is' and 'No t'isn't', glaring through a mask of dough from a half-chewed sandwich!

Above right Donald Beale and Peter Smith at Branksome. *(Date: 23 May 1985.)*

Right Donald Beale and Peter Smith inspect the disused viaduct of the Bournemouth West curve. *(Date: 23 May 1985.)*

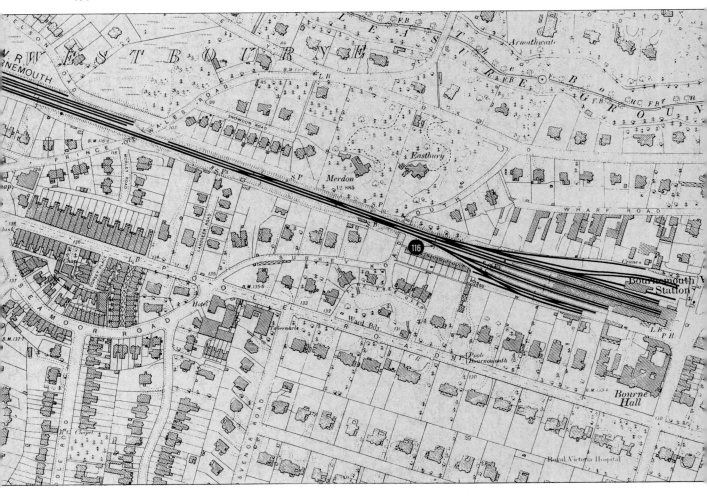

Map 30, 1902: Bournemouth West

The terminus for S&D trains, 71½ miles from Bath. The station had six platforms provided with ample canopies, but no overall roof.

The layout remained the same as this map suggests, with only minor detail alterations taking place over the years, until the station's closure upon electrification of the Waterloo to Bournemouth Line in 1965. S&D trains were never again to use its facilities after 2 August of that year, being diverted to Bournemouth Central. However some trains started and terminated at Branksome Station. The official date of closure for Bournemouth West was 4 October 1965.

Today the A35 by-pass (Wessex Way) cuts across the area east/west and just yards to the north of the station site itself, (now a coach and car park) and then runs parallel with the old railway. However the Midland Hotel, once a familiar landmark, still survives!

The carriage cleaning plant still has a siding supplied with a third rail which continues on over the old Surrey Road Bridge, where it ends.

116
Bournemouth West
(195 SY 074 915)

BR Class '5' 4-6-0 No 73052, then only three months old, sets off from Bournemouth West with the 18.40 for Bath.

The layout of the station can be judged well from this photograph. The platform canopies are shown to good effect and over them can be seen the roof of the Midland Hotel. *(Photo: Ivo Peters. Date: 7 August 1954.)*

The same view today shows the A35 cutting across the site of the old station, leaving the Midland Hotel in the background to provide the familiar backdrop.

The siding on the left is the last railway link and marks the end of the carriage shed and cleaning plant layout, further up the track. *(Date: 23 May 1985.)*

Chapter 10
Pylle—Edington Junction

117
Pylle (183 ST 618 389)

This view of Pylle Station, shows the seventeen-lever signal box which had closed in 1929, the passing loop being removed at the same time. The remaining siding to the attractive stone goods shed was controlled by a ground frame to which the signal box had become relegated, before being finally demolished around 1965 upon closure of the siding in 1963. An interesting feature is that the eastern end of the goods shed was the station master's house.

The station, built adjacent to the Fosse Way, was at least a mile from the village it served. *(Photo: Lens of Sutton. Date: 1961)*

The goods shed has now been converted into a meat packing centre. The site was up for sale during my visit here. The station building remains remarkably intact and the central door is still clearly marked 'Booking Office'. The 'Up' platform has been 'chewed' somewhat, but again remains largely intact. The road bridge carrying the A37 Fosse Way has been demolished.

Left The door of the station building, still clearly marked 'BOOKING OFFICE'. *(Date: 16 May 1985.)*

118

West Pennard
(182/183 ST 568 395)

Class '3F' No 43216 gets away from West Pennard with a Highbridge to Evercreech local.

West Pennard was the first block post and crossing place after Evercreech Junction, since Pylle ceased to be such in 1929. At this point the line started its journey across the flatlands of Somerset and ran dead straight for four miles to the bridge over the A39 near Glastonbury (S&D No 264) which survives today. The large stone-built goods shed and seven-ton hand crane were served by a lengthy double-ended siding. The stone station building had the usual facilities of a booking office and a waiting room.

The station, like a few others on the branch, was some distance from the village it served, being two miles away. However, it was well laid out and neatly contained. This photograph was taken from the A361 road bridge (S&D No 257). *(Photo: The late Derek Cross, via D. M. Cross. Date: 29 June 1962.)*

Despite the growth on the track-bed, the buildings remain in remarkable condition and like Pylle, the site was up for sale at the time of my visit. The goods shed has been converted for use as a small industrial unit and is in very good order, both externally and internally.

The station building is a gem and has virtually remained untouched for twenty years. The booking hall and office still have BR notices on the walls. The fireplaces remain intact, as do the lavatories in the waiting room and on the platform.

The booking office still has all its shelves and cupboards, as if it were only vacated yesterday. However, one or two floorboards are suspect —a heavyweight like myself has to tread very carefully! The main A361 road was realigned many years ago and the railway bridge was removed.

Right Still on the wall of the booking office after twenty years of disuse, a crumbling notice bears witness to the traffic of years past. *(Date: 15 June 1985.)*

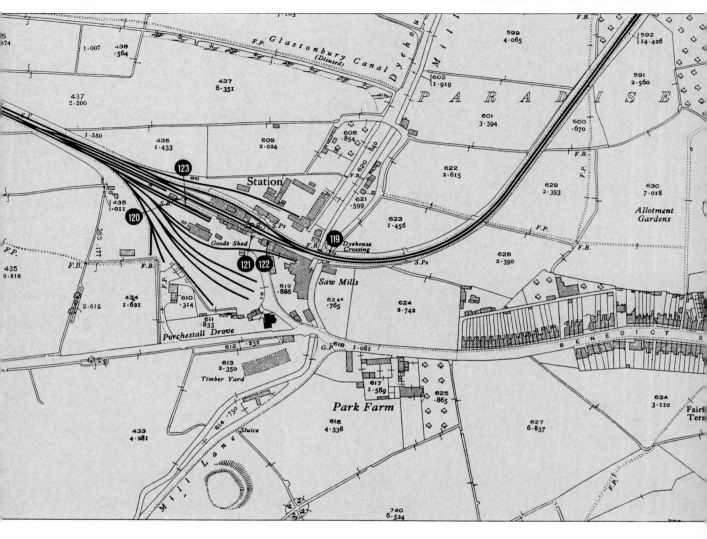

Map 31, 1930 (east)/1904 (west): Glastonbury

Highlighted on this map is 'The Pollards', built in 1861 as the Abbey Arms and Railway Hotel, part of which was leased to the Somerset Central Railway as offices. The S&D continued to use them until 1877 for the same purpose. The quadrangle of buildings on the north side were of single storey wooden construction and used as engineers' workshops.

The station buildings were of simple wooden construction with large canopies. A splendid covered footbridge linked the 'Up' platform to the island platforms, the north face of which was used by trains for the Wells branch until its closure in 1951. The line for the Wells branch ran parallel around the 9½-chain radius curve, with the one to Evercreech Junction before parting after a mile or so to the north-east.

The goods yard was spacious and provided with two cranes, shed and cattle loading docks and was the scene of considerable activity during its life. The substantial 29-lever signal box was strategically placed off the west end of the 'Up' platform.

The saw mills and timber yard still operate—trading as John Snow & Co Ltd. Note the disused Glastonbury Canal which terminated here. The station remained intact until it was dismantled in 1984. The island platform canopy has been re-erected in Glastonbury's open air market under the auspices of the Manpower Services Commission.

119
Glastonbury, Dyehouse Lane Crossing
(182/183 ST 491 389)

A Whit Monday excursion from Weston-super-Mare to Bournemouth gets under way from Glastonbury, hauled by '4F' 0-6-0 No 44417 sending a towering plume of exhaust high in the air, as it is about to pass over Dyehouse Lane crossing.

The disused portion of the bridge, over a stream parallel to the road, in the foreground used to carry the Wells branch line before it was dismantled, following closure in 1951. The ornate footbridge of Glastonbury Station is just visible over the train. The hopper is that of the adjacent saw mills. *(Photo: David Milton. Date: 1961.)*

Today the crossing is fenced off but the old bridge over the stream is unchanged. The crossing gate posts still stand on either side of the lane. Notice that the saw mill's hopper has been traded in for a smaller model! *(Date: 15 May 1985.)*

120
Glastonbury and Street Station (182 ST 490 390)

A panoramic view taken from the signal box of Glastonbury and Street Station, showing clearly the generous proportions of the station.

The buildings were of wooden construction with fine canopies linked at the eastern end by an elegant footbridge with a latticed lower section and covered top. The island 'Down' platform on the left of the picture could even boast a refreshment room at one time! The engineers' workshops can be seen behind the island canopy on the left and formed a quadrangle. The north face of the island platform was used by Wells branch line trains until its closure in 1951. The main booking hall and waiting rooms are on the 'Up' platform on the right.

Glastonbury Tor is clearly visible in the background of this interesting photograph. *(Photo: R. E. Toop. Date: 13 June 1959.)*

Remarkably, the station remained intact until mid 1984 when British Rail issued a contract for the demolition of the buildings to platform level.

An imaginative £52,000 scheme was proposed by the Mendip District Council (MDC) in conjunction with the Somerset County Council Probation Service Community Programme (PSCP) and the Manpower Service Commission (MSC) to dismantle the island platform canopy and re-erect it at a car park in Glastonbury Town centre, also the site of an open air market. The PSCP provided the management and labour, whilst the MSC and MDC and a conservation society paid the wages.

The one-year contract started mid 1984, the buildings were gradually dismantled and all salvageable materials were stored in the goods shed prior to transportation and re-erection. A small building just east of the goods shed was refurbished for use as a mess room by the PSCP labour force. The major work of dismantling had to be completed by the autumn of 1984 to take advantage of the weather before the onset of winter, when conditions would become difficult.

After a period of uncertainty brought about by the year's contract with the PSCP being due to expire and delays caused by British Rail selling all the metal (including the goods shed) remaining on the site, the PSCP had to move all salvaged materials to a new site near the town centre. However by May 1985 the re-erection work on the car park site was under way. The footings had been dug for the supporting timber pillars which were renewed. The Somerset and Dorset Railway Trust were consulted regarding the correct colour scheme and Glastonbury now sports a newly refurbished station building.

This photograph shows the dereliction following the removal of the materials from the site. (Unfortunately a very untidy mess was left on and behind the platforms.) Note the old engineers' offices on the left, now used as dwellings. *(Date: 31 May 1985.)*

Below left The demolition of the booking office underway. *(Date: 23 July 1984.)*

121
Glastonbury (182 ST 491 389)

Class '3F' 0-6-0 No 43218 setting off from Glastonbury and Street Station with a Highbridge to Templecombe train. Note Glastonbury Tor visible in the background.

Of interest is the notice on the shed, showing 'Southern' influence! The line, seen curving sharply in the background, had a 5 mph speed restriction for 9½ chains and skirted Glastonbury to take it right round the town's northern side before heading east towards Evercreech. The Wells branch ran parallel to it for about a mile, the lines then diverging to the north of the town. *(Photo: R. E. Toop. Date: 13 June 1959.)*

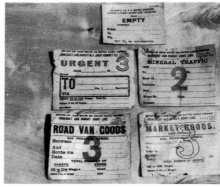

The track-bed is still visible, but rather overgrown. The shed that was in the foreground was demolished in 1984. The small trees have all but obscured the view to Glastonbury Tor, however the Nissen hut alongside the track is still visible. *(Date: 25 June 1985.)*

Above Labels found in the shed, pictured in the foreground of the 1959 picture, during demolition, July 1984.

Cole Station (183 ST 671 334)

The rather grubby BR Class '4' No 75072 departs from Cole with the 13.10 Bath–Templecombe 'Down' local.

Cole was particularly photogenic in railway terms and was able to provide great variety as such. The neat and tidy station and small goods yard could be viewed well from this bridge, which provided an excellent vantage point from which to photograph trains. Cole Viaduct was also well within view from here. *(Photo: R. C. Riley (6604). Date: 1 September 1962.)*

The dark, satanic sky, heavily laden with rain, provides the backdrop to Cole Station today; the scudding clouds part just enough to allow the buildings to be briefly illuminated by sunshine before the onset of another squally shower. Some rubble and spoil from Cole Viaduct can be seen on the track-bed in untidy piles. *(Date: 5 November 1985.)*

Wincanton (183 ST 710 282)

Class '7F' No 53810, in charge of an engineers' train consisting of a mess coach and ballast wagons, stands patiently at Wincanton on a Sunday whilst maintenance is undertaken on the running lines through the station.

The goods shed stands adjacent to the 'Down' line and directly opposite the 'Up' platform. The platforms were staggered, which did not enhance either the station's aesthetics or ergonomics!

The large 'Cow & Gate' milk factory at Wincanton is just visible in front of the engine. *(Photo: R. C. Riley (5468). Date: 16 July 1961.)*

A Westerly gale endeavours to blow the leaves from young trees that now grow on the track-bed which has been grassed over and landscaped. Trees have been planted from just south of the old 'Up' platform right back to the parapets of the bridge that used to span the A303 (Bridge 137). Today the 'Unigate' factory has expanded – its buildings now occupy the area upon which the goods shed once stood. *(Date: 5 November 1985.)*

Templecombe
(183 ST 709 228)

Class '4F' 0-6-0 No 44559 heads past Templecombe shed, with the 16.16 Evercreech Junction to Bournemouth, and on towards Henstridge.

This splendid photograph was taken from the platform of a triple function signal located adjacent to the 'Up' line halfway along the spur to Templecombe Upper Station. It provides a panoramic view of the shed, Templecombe Lower platform and the SR line, plus the spur to the Upper Station seen on the right.

Templecombe Lower can be spotted between Combe Throop Road Bridge (No 152) and the SR line bridge (No 153). The platform was last used by 'Up' trains on 3 January 1966. It was built in 1887 when trains ceased to use the old Dorset Central Station, the remaining buildings of which are visible adjacent to the locomotives standing in the siding alongside the shed. *(Photo: R. C. Riley (3904). Date: 12 July 1960.)*

The old spur to Templecombe Upper has been made into a slip road to the factory site now located here, which has meant some 20ft of embankment being removed to provide sensible access to it.

The changes are all too obvious, but the shed still has a useful part to play as part of the site complex. The factory, owned by the giant Plessey Group, has provided employment for many ex-railway staff over the years since the S&D's closure. Ex-railway staff that still work there include: Jim Young – Guard – (1944–66) Reg Brewer – Guard – (1941–66) Bruce Briant – Fireman – (1961–66) Rodney Scovell – Driver – (1947–63) Margaret Moore – Buffet – (8 years in the '40s & '50s) Les Davis – Carriage & Wagon Department I am particularly grateful to the Plessey Group and staff for their help in allowing me to photograph from the site on several occasions. *(Date: 12 November 1985.)*

Sturminster Newton Bridge over the River Stour (No 171)
(194 ST 783 143)

'9F' No 92220 *Evening Star* rumbles back over the River Stour bridge, just north of Sturminster Newton, with the 15.40 Bournemouth to Bristol 'Up Mail', having worked the 09.55 semi-fast from Bath to Bournemouth earlier in the day. *Evening Star* was specially transferred to Bath MPD on 8 August 1962 in order that it would be available to work the last 'Pines Express'. One week after this photograph was taken, the last 'Pines Express' ran over S&D metals (on 8 September 1962). *Evening Star* was transferred away from Bath MPD a few days later, on 13 September.

However, a year later, the ridiculous spectacle of seeing this magnificent engine hauling three or four coach local trains up and down the line, was an insult to its capabilities: due to locomotive shortage it had been transferred back to the system for a short period, the line by then being run purely as a local service. *(Photo: R. C. Riley (6612). Date: 1 September 1962.)*

The River Stour is quite unchanged by the passage of time as it flows on its unhurried course to the sea. The girder bridge has been demolished, but the brick arches remain and are likely to provide a reminder of a great past for some considerable time into the future. *(Date: 6 November 1985.)*

122
Glastonbury
(182 ST 491 389)

A double-headed train hauled by '4F' 0-6-0 No 44560 and a BR Standard Class 3 2-6-2T leaves Glastonbury for Evercreech and the south, shrouding the footbridge in steam. Two amused onlookers on the right 'watch the birdie' and get into the picture! Note the smartly attired station staff. *(Photo: David Milton. Date: 1960.)*

After the bomb? Glastonbury has received attention from the scrap men, who were contracted to remove all the metal available. All buildings have been demolished, leaving this untidy mess. However, the island canopy has now been re-erected at Glastonbury's Open Air Market and car park. *(Date: 15 May 1985).*

123

Glastonbury Goods Yard and Signal Box (182 ST 490 390)

The attractive 29-lever wooden signal box commands an excellent view of the goods yard to either side of it. Glastonbury goods yard was large and well laid out and usually busy. Seen here is ex-GWR 0-6-0 No 2218 indulging in some shunting before proceeding with an east-bound goods. *(Photo: Ivo Peters. Date: 8 October 1964.)*

A scrap merchant has recently deposited the pile of metal here. The area in the background has been used by John Snow's timber yard for many years as a site for the burning of waste materials from the saw mill operations.

The footings of the old signal box can still be made out on the left of the picture. Just a small portion of the platform is visible in the foreground. Just out of sight to the left is the remains of the one-ton hand

crane: the column and pulley wheel stand forlornly amongst the dereliction. The seven-ton crane column survives in the yard, as do the old cattle pens. *(Date: 17 June 1985.)*

Above right The remains of the one-ton crane echo the towers of St John's Church and Glastonbury Tor, representing, in its own way, just as valid a part of history as the two much older monuments. *(Date: 17 June 1985.)*

124
Ashcott Station
(182 ST 449 397)

The simple concrete platform of the station replaced an earlier wooden structure and had no facilities on it. The booking office and waiting room was annexed to Station House adjacent to the Ashcott to Meare Road. The small goods yard controlled by a ground frame was on the west side of the station and the road. The station was an inconvenient 2¼ miles from Ashcott village. *(Photo: David Milton. Date: June 1960.)*

Archie Attwell, who was the latter day Ashcott porter and still lives here, prepares to move his car in order that I can photograph the station site. However he is more photogenic than the hedge behind him which hides the remaining sections of platform supports and posts, and I include him for some human interest in this uninspiring scene. *(Date: 31 May 1985)*

Above right Station House is suffering from subsidence, probably due to the Sedgemoor South Drain running east/west directly behind the building. *(Date: July 1984.)*
Right A familiar sight to Archie Attwell: Ashcott Station crossing gates and ground frame. *(Photo: David Milton. Date: 1961.)*

125
Shapwick Station
(182 ST 423 412)

Shapwick was a block post with a lengthy crossing loop and two sidings on the 'Up' side to the east of the station, which was situated 2¼ miles north of Shapwick village.

The wooden signal box of seventeen levers stood adjacent to the crossing which it controlled and was used until closure of the line in 1966.

The 'Up' platform had a simple wooden building with two waiting rooms and a booking office, whilst the 'Down' side had no buildings or shelter. Peat traffic was a major source of revenue here in the first quarter of this century, but road traffic gradually eroded this. *(Photo: David Milton. Date: 10 June 1960.)*

Absolutely nothing remains. The South Drain seen on the left has been widened, the bridge has been replaced and in turn displaced the site of the signal box.

Above right The only vestige that does give a hint of the former role of the area is the gate of the goods yard on the east side of the road. Near to this site are the recently discovered remains of a neolithic walkway. *(Date: 15 May 1985.)*

Right The old peat railway loading platform adjacent to Alexander's siding between Ashcott and Shapwick. The former S&DJR branch line ran just the other side of the ramp. *(Date: May 1985)*

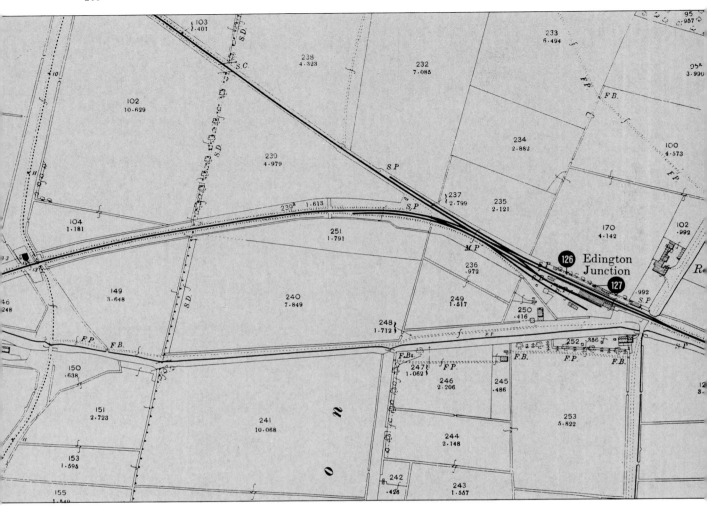

Map 32, 1904: Edington Junction

Edington Road Station opened in 1856 to serve the villages of Edington and Burtle, some 2½ miles apart. Like other stations on the Somerset levels, it was rather remote, but achieved higher status by becoming Edington Junction in 1890 upon the opening of the Bridgwater Branch.

The layout was fairly comprehensive — the 'Up' platform became an island with the south face of it providing access for the Bridgwater

Branch trains. The station building, of wooden construction, was at the eastern end of the 'Up' platform, which also had a large canopy extending to half its length. The 'Down' platform housed a wooden shelter and staff rooms which fell into disrepair and were demolished following the closure of the Bridgwater Branch for passengers in 1952. The charming 39-lever wooden signal box, situated off the west end of the island platform, also closed that year and was soon demolished along with most of the sidings and the 'Down' crossing

loop. The remaining siding was then controlled by a ground frame.

The station was renamed Edington Burtle in 1953 and the Bridgwater Branch continued to be used by goods traffic until final closure in October 1954.

Of interest is the level crossing keeper's cottage seen highlighted on the left of the map which controlled the gates over Goose Lane on the Bridgwater Branch—it survives today. The Railway Hotel has been renamed 'The Tom Mogg Inn' after one of the station's latter-day signalmen.

126
Edington Junction (1)
(182 ST 392 428)

This view of Edington Junction looking towards Glastonbury shows the generous proportions of this remote station prior to removal of the loop and 'Down' platform. The wooden station buildings and the large island canopy can be seen clearly in this photograph. The Bridgwater Branch trains used the south face of the island platform in the background. Note the interesting shunting signal seen just over the 'Down' platform's shelter.

Two anecdotes relating to Edington Junction are worthy of telling. The first involved driver George Wheadon who was proceeding with an 'Up' goods one dark and blustery night when he was halted by the signalman at Edington who officiously informed him that his engine was not showing a light (which had obviously blown out), and he was not to proceed until it had been re-lit. George, knowing how futile this would be, told the signalman in no uncertain terms what he could do with the light, and opening the regulator blasted on through the station and on his way!

The other tale involves Horace Pople, a relief porter from Bridgwater, who was despatched by bicycle from Bridgwater to Edington in a raging blizzard. One duty was to close the crossing gates over the road. It was usual practice for the signalman at Edington to close the gates (which was only three minutes' work) so the relief porter could catch the last train back to Bridgwater. On this occasion the signalman refused to do this, so poor Horace Pople had to watch the last train disappear round the bend west of the station to Bridgwater and attend to his duty before cycling back home to Bridgwater in the blizzard! *(Photo: via Will Locke. Date: summer 1951.)*

Brambles are winning the day, but the island platform survives, although it has been reduced in length by 100 feet or so to make way for the garden and drive of Station House. The goods yard gate survives in poor condition, but Station House, seen to the left and now a private dwelling, has been magnificently restored. *(Date: 24 May 1985.)*

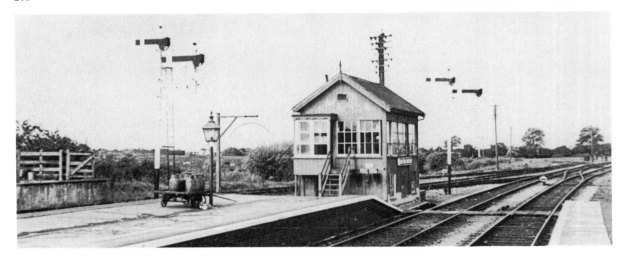

127
Edington Junction (2)
(182 ST 392 428)

Pictured here is the most attractive 39-lever wooden signal box situated off the end of the island platform at the west end of the station. The box controlled the branch for Bridgwater, seen curving to the left in the distance, also the adjacent goods yard. The cattle pens are just visible on the left of the picture. The light on the platform and trolley underneath with a number of milk churns complete this picturesque scene.

The lines of the Burnham and Bridgwater branches ran parallel from Edington Station before diverging some six chains west of the island platform. This was on occasions the scene of friendly rivalry. A Bridgwater branch train, having waited for the arrival of an Evercreech to Highbridge connection, was able to race it away from the station, resulting in spectacular performances from both engines as their crews vied for the lead over the few chains before they went their separate ways! *(Photo: via Will Locke. Date: pre 1951.)*

The land is now owned by the Wessex Water Board. The 'Up' platform on the left has all but succumbed to brambles, whilst the remains of the 'Down' platform, now an untidy pile or rubble, has become completely overgrown.

Still seen clearly is the old base of the cattle pen. The excavator in the background has been preparing the ground for the erection of an agricultural building. A little way to the south-west of the station on the old Bridgwater Branch at Goose Lane crossing an old keeper's cottage still survives. *(Date: 24 May 1985.)*

128
Huntspill Crossing
(182 ST 372 444)

One of the idiosyncrasies of the branch line was that water had to be delivered to some crossing keepers' cottages in the remote areas of the moor!

This crossing, mid point between Edington and Bason Bridge, was one such case. Seen here are the crew of ex-GWR 0-6-0 No 3206 with an 'Up' goods, making such a stop to unload the small churns of water for the level crossing keeper's cottage which was located beyond the far side of the tender. *(Photo: R. E. Toop. Date: 16 June 1962.)*

A few vestiges remain of the level crossing. The posts are a familiar pointer. Some iron bracing off one of the gates can be seen discarded next to the old kissing gate. The crossing keeper's cottage—always very damp because of the high water table—has long since been demolished.

This photograph shows the remote area to advantage with the distant Mendip Hills seen in the background. *(Date: 5 March 1985.)*

Chapter 11
Bason Bridge— Burnham-on- Sea

129
Bason Bridge milk factory
(182 ST 348 457)

The main activity at Bason Bridge was until recently, the milk factory— then owned by United Dairies. Prenationalization, the milk traffic for London was routed via Templecombe and after via the Western Region, to the greater extent.

Seen here is Class '4F' 0-6-0 No 44272 leaving Bason Bridge with a milk train. The River Brue is in the foreground. The siding was controlled by the 'east' ground frame, seen in the middle of the picture. *(Photo: R. E. Toop. Date: 18 May 1963.)*

The milk traffic lasted until 2 October 1972, some years after the closure of the branch. A probable reason for this traffic ceasing may have been the construction of the M5 motorway 1½ miles to the west of Bason Bridge but road transport was on the increase and therefore to continue the link, involving expensive construction of a new rail bridge and bank formation to elevate the line over the M5, was not practical.

The factory has expanded greatly as can be judged by this photograph which was only taken after a lot of bramble hacking and pruning! Recently, however, Dairy Crest have announced that the factory is to close. *(Date: 1 May 1985.)*

130
Bason Bridge Station
(182 ST 345 458)

A nice view of Bason Bridge Station with its neat and tidy wooden buildings at the far end of the platform, beyond which is the B3141 road. The crossing gates were controlled from the west ground frame seen opposite the far end of the platform. The milk factory chimney looks a bit out from the perpendicular! *(Photo: David Milton. Date: 10 June 1960.)*

Only the platform survives and even it is overgrown with brambles.

The large building of the modern milk factory can be seen for miles around the area and stands out like a sore thumb! I think it could well benefit from the talents of a commissioned graffiti artist to see if it can be blended into the landscape a little better than it is! *(Date: 23 April 1985.)*

Map 33, 1904: Highbridge (East)

The prominent feature on the map is the Locomotive and Carriage Works which was the headquarters for the repair of locomotives and rolling stock since this was the original main line for the S&D.

Three small outside cylinder saddle tanks specially designed to work at Radstock (under 'Marble Arch') were built here, No 25a (0-4-2T) in 1885, and No 26a and 45a (0-4-0Ts) in 1895. These earned the nickname of *'Dazzlers'* due to their standard of cleanliness in the early days. Highbridge Works was closed in 1930 and some 300 men were made redundant—a bitter blow to a small town—mainly brought about as an economy measure forced by the ever-increasing threat of road transport.

Highbridge Station had a total of seven platforms, two of which served the GWR/Bristol & Exeter Railway at the northern end of which the S&D line crossed at 45°

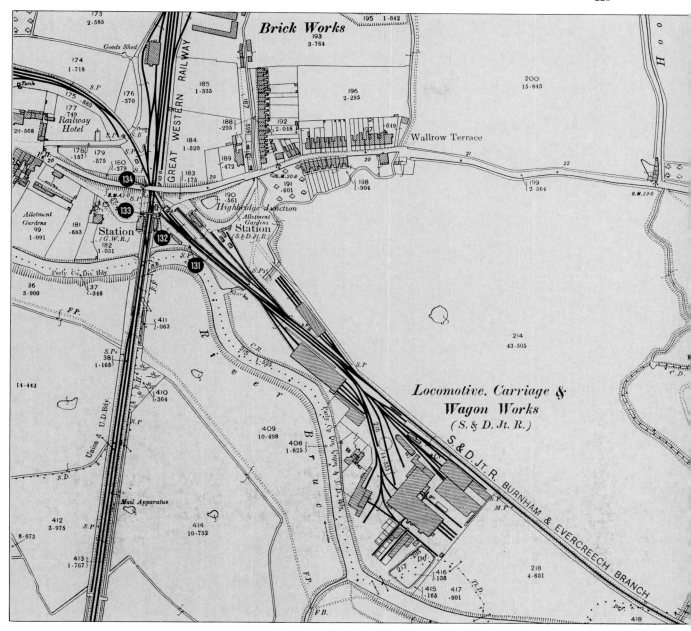

underneath a road bridge curving westwards around towards the town centre. This crossing was controlled by the GWR box situated at the north end of the 'Down' GWR platform after 1914. Directly opposite this box, across the S&D track, was the diminutive 'A' Box which jointly controlled the crossing prior to that date. The station buildings were of brick construction with stone facings. Today the S&D station and works site is a wasteland and up for sale for development as an industrial site. Only a section of the 'Up' platform remains and the engine house of the gas station.

The old GWR station lost its buildings two or three years ago, when they were replaced by two modern 'bus shelter' types.

131
Highbridge (East)
(182 ST 323 469)

Signs of activity! Often the station was not busy in its latter days. The 13.15 from Evercreech Junction has just arrived on the 'Up' platform and disgorges its passengers whilst Ivatt 2-6-2T No 41249 prepares to depart with the 14.20 to Evercreech.

Highbridge (East) could boast five platforms seen here, two served a bay in which the Ivatt is standing. The diminutive Highbridge 'A' box closed in 1914 and seen in front of the concrete footbridge, served as a mess room for many years. *Photo: The late Derek Cross, via D. M. Cross. Date: October 1965.)*

The black bridge over the Western Region main line stands the test of time, whilst all about has been torn asunder!

The last section of concrete 'Up' platform and bridge remains, but the area in the foreground has been used to tip building rubble and looks untidy. *(Date: 1 May 1985.)*

Above The last service train to leave Highbridge for Templecombe and return prepares to depart as driver Clarence Rawles adjusts his charge '2MT' No 41249. *(Photo: David Milton. Date: 5 March 1966.)*

132
Highbridge (East)
(182 ST 322 470)

This excellent view taken from the footbridge gives an idea of the extensive layout of the station and its five platforms. The brick station building provided the only shelter on this vast expanse! Seen in the background are the sheds and old works (closed 1930). The line in the immediate foreground crossed the GWR main line at 45° to Highbridge Wharf and Burnham-on-Sea. *(Photo: David Milton. Date: July 1960.)*

This wilderness is all that remains. During the construction of the M5 motorway, which required many thousands of tons of ballast for the flatlands across which it was being built, a new spur was connected from the 'Down' Western main line to provide access to this site and the former branch line. This involved erecting a temporary Bailey bridge just to the east of the original black bridge (S&D No 281) under which the new spur passed. Class '37' diesels working in pairs hauled slag from South Wales. Trains climbed a newly-built embankment to discharge their loads over a screen in similar fashion to the merry-go-round principle used at power stations, except that a run round loop was built enabling the train to be hauled back out from whence it came.

The last rails were lifted a few years ago, the temporary bridge having been removed some time before and the road was made good again. The 25.7-acre site is currently up for sale for industrial development and offers are sought in the region of £500,000! *(Date: 23 April 1985.)*

133
Highbridge Crossover
(182 ST 322 470)

Ex-LMS '8F' 2-8-0 No 48309 draws into Highbridge (GWR) from Bath via Mangotsfield and Bristol with an RCTS special. This loco was allocated to Bath and was one of only two fitted with steam heating apparatus. On the right is the GWR wedge-shaped signal box which controlled the S&D crossing (seen under the loco). The black bridge carries the B3139 road. *(Photo: Ivo Peters. Date: 2 January 1966.)*

A Bristol Temple Meads to Taunton DMU draws into Highbridge Station, a complete contrast in terms of 'exciting' motive power!

The signal box has long since been removed, as has the goods yard and the S&D crossing it controlled. Of interest are the facing crossover points which were in the process of being repaired. *(Date: 1 May 1985.)*

134
Highbridge (East) 'B' Box
(182 ST 322 471)

This photograph is a real feast for the eyes! Like many railway scenes of yesteryear, it has splendid variety. The small twelve-lever 'B' Box is on the left and controls the entrance to the goods yard (further to the left out of sight) and the crossing seen adjacent to it. Beyond the signals in a siding are a couple of engineers' wagons, with oil drums in one of them. The corrugated iron hut in the foreground was apparently an oil store. Will Locke told me that a lad was locked in here for a joke, which nearly turned sour as he almost suffocated with the fumes which were exacerbated by the stifling conditions experienced inside. *(Photo: David Milton. Date: July 1960.)*

This photograph had to be taken from a new pedestrian bridge erected on the north side of the B3139 road bridge spanning the WR main line, so I was slightly forward of the position adopted by David Milton in taking the 1960 picture.

The corrugated hut remains, but little else. How bland the same scene is today—even the GW goods yard and its shed has gone! At least the HST 125, Plymouth-bound, breaks up the monotony (top right). The BR vehicles to the right belonged to engineers repairing the crossover point-work just off the station platforms. *(Date: 1 May 1985.)*

Map 34, 1930: Highbridge Wharf

Highbridge Wharf was situated west of Highbridge Station. Access was gained by a crossing over a main road (A38) controlled by the delightful Highbridge 'C' Box, renamed 'Highbridge East "A"' in BR days.

The wharf was, for almost a century, a busy scene. Coal, timber and rails were some of the cargoes handled. The S&D owned its own ships, finally disposing of the two remaining vessels in 1933–4 upon the winding up of their shipping interests. The wharf continued to be used by private shipping until 1950 or so.

The saw mill is now part of a large builders merchants—Jewsons —previously trading as John Bland & Co. The Glastonbury Canal terminated near here, access to which was through the gates of a sea lock at the eastern end of the wharf. Today the wharves are finally being filled in—only a small section can still be seen at the time of writing.

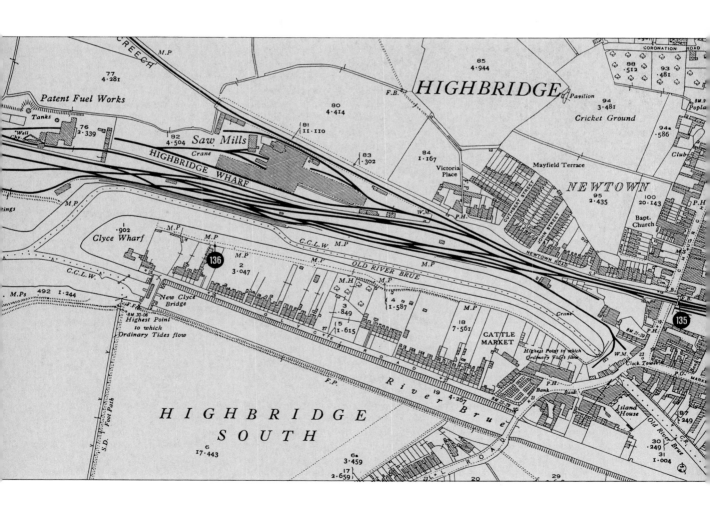

135
Highbridge Wharf (1)
(182 ST 320 472)

The attractive Highbridge East 'A' signal box with its delightful balustrade controlled the crossing over the busy A38 road in the foreground, also the wharf line and Burnham branch seen swinging to the right. The roofs of holiday-makers' cars are seen crossing over the railway line. Highbridge was a notorious bottleneck for holiday traffic in the days before the M5 motorway.

Again this picture is full of variety —obviously the old gentleman leaning on the crossing gate thought there was plenty to look at! Notice the signalman walking back down the line to his box; he most probably had been along the wharf to have a chat with somebody seen standing in the distance! The pub on the left proudly displays the black horse symbol of Starkey's Ales—this was a well-known West Country Brewery, now absorbed by the giant Whitbread Group. *(Photo: David Milton. Date: July 1960.)*

The butcher's boy has grown a little older now! He has got DIY commitments, no doubt to fix that long overdue shelf for the wife! The egg advert may be rather prophetic if he fails to get the job done on time!

This photograph was taken from a supermarket's upstairs window (kindly held open by the manager) whilst I waited for the scudding clouds to clear before taking this photograph—which is full of coincidences. How many people can you see that are in approximately the same position as 25 years before?—quite uncanny.

The pub that was on the left is now a guest house. The A38 road is much quieter these days as the volume of traffic has gone to the M5. *(Date: 20 April 1985.)*

"He was everything I wanted but now he's had his chips"

136
Highbridge Wharf (2)
(182 ST 314 473)

The 195-ton *Radstock* was owned by the S&D and joined the fleet in 1925 to replace the *Alpha* which was sucked into the mud at No 2 berth—failing to rise on the tide. She was unfortunately carrying 130 tons of flour at the time!

Radstock is having her cargo of coal unloaded into a hotch potch of trucks at the wharf side. The S&D wound up their shipping interests in 1933 and subsequently the *Radstock* was sold. *(Photo: British Rail [Railprint]. Date: late 1920s.)*

Jewson time! The vandal caught in the act, as the old wharf gradually disappears under the infilling. The shed in the background belongs to the adjacent timber yard and that well-known builders' merchant! *(Date: 15 May 1985.)*

Map 35, 1903:
Burnham-on-Sea

The station opened after the 1¾ mile extension from Highbridge was completed in 1858.

As befitting a terminus, it was supplied with a train shed, having an overall roof under which it had the usual facilities, plus a small goods yard nearby complete with a small signal box. The roof afforded some protection from the offshore gales blowing across the nearby Bristol Channel!

A 1-in-23 incline took the line out onto a pier extending some way into the estuary of the River Parrett. The pier was used by shipping for a limited time, trucks being hauled up and down the gradient by wire-ropes.

Alongside the station building can be seen the lifeboat station which had its own siding down which the lifeboat could be launched off the end of the pier! The lifeboat was removed in 1930: the railway station closed on 29 October 1951 although holiday excursions continued until 8 September 1962.

Today the station site forms part of a new road, but the lifeboat house survives as a Scout hut. The pier is now used to launch pleasure craft. The Queen's Hotel still occupies its rightful position on the promenade. The nearby Somerset & Dorset Hotel is now resplendent in a new coat of paint and well painted signs commemorating the railway of the same name, survive!

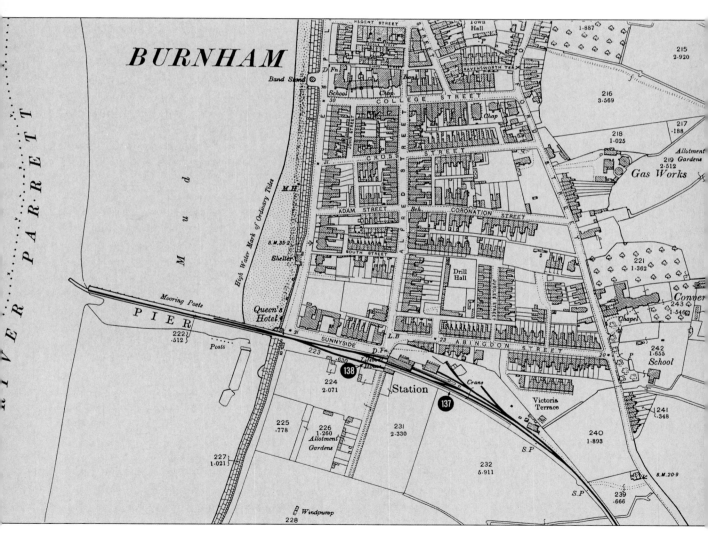

137
Burnham-on-Sea (1)
(182 ST 305 488)

A nice study of Burnham Station on a sleepy summer's afternoon. The overall roof is seen, which made the station building rather dark. The tiny four-lever signal box stands at the eastern end of the platform.

This photograph was taken from the excursion platform which was built at a later date. The Queen's Hotel is behind the station roof and stands on the sea front promenade.

The late John Betjeman's film of a trip from Evercreech terminated here and he was finally seen skipping across Burnham sands in front of the hotel, issuing edicts to Dr Beeching! *(Photo: R. E. Toop. Date: 22 August 1959.)*

The Queen's Hotel and the house in the foreground provide the clues! A new road has been built, following the old route of the track bed for some way out of the town, and saves considerable time getting to the sea front from outlying areas. *(Date: 20 April 1985.)*

Left 'The Somerset & Dorset' public house adjacent to the station site. *(Date: 24 May 1985.)*

138
Burnham-on-Sea (2)
(182 ST 304 487)

Class '3F' 0-6-0 No 43427 pokes her nose out from Burnham's overall roof, after having arrived with a summer excursion. The 'Black and White' coach on the left conjures up many childhood memories for me. They were seen all over the West Country at that time. The coach is a Bristol LGG type with Duplex bodywork and was one of a second batch delivered in 1948 (withdrawn in 1960-61).

The old lifeboat house is just visible on the extreme right of the picture. *(Photo: R. E. Toop. Date: 22 August 1959.)*

I never thought that I would see fit to take a photograph of a telephone box—especially a modern type! However the evening sky provides a dramatic backdrop to the location of what was the former railway station. Note the Scout hut on the right. *(Date: 24 May 1985.)*

Chapter 12
Bridgwater and Wells Branches

139
Cossington Bank and Board's Siding
(182 ST 363 408)

This climb of the Polden Hills, on a rising gradient of 1:72 for about a mile, would, on occasions, be the downfall of an Edington to Bridgwater goods, which could not quite make it to Cossington. It then had to reverse all the way down again in order to have another 'stab' at it!

Class '2P' S&D No 70 still in her Prussian Blue livery climbs up Cossington Bank to have her photograph taken whilst undergoing a trial on the Bridgwater branch. However, Class '2P's were seldom seen on the line, so this event apparently came to nothing!

The cutting to Board's Siding is just visible on the right of the picture. The siding served a quarry which provided the branch with good revenue until 1933 when it closed. Glastonbury Tor is seen on the horizon. *(Photo: British Rail [Railprint]. Date: circa 1924–25.)*

In recent years the area has been used as a council tip, now fortunately closed. To find the exact location of this facsimile, I noticed a triangulated concrete post in the original photograph, so I set about looking for it further down the field. Having located it, I then traced back through the undergrowth the appropriate number of posts I had counted in the original photograph! So here it is—Glastonbury Tor included! The Mendip Hills are seen in the distance. *(Date: 31 May 1985.)*

140
Cossington Station
(182 ST 357 408)

Class '3F' 0-6-0 No 43216 on the 10.38 Bridgwater to Edington Junction pauses at Cossington and waits whilst its photograph is taken!

The substantial grey freestone station master's house dominates this country station and almost dwarfs the annexe which housed the booking office and two waiting rooms. The ground frame seen on the station platform controlled a siding which served cattle pens and an end loading dock. Cattle traffic was substantial at one time, animals being freighted to the markets at Highbridge and Bridgwater.

One quaint note in the Somerset & Dorset working timetables stated: 'All engines working passenger trains not running funnel first must stop at Cossington, whether marked to do so or not'. This station closed to passenger traffic on 1 December 1952. *(Photo: via Douglas Allen, Date: 1 March 1952.)*

A family connection with Cossington Station enabled me to ask whether it would be in order to do some hedge laying so that I might be able to take a photograph of the old station! Given the go-ahead I scythed my way through elm, elder and brambles for at least 20 feet or more. Two hours' backbreaking work plus one completely torn pair of trousers later, I was able to get this shot of the building!

The platform is quite distinct and now supports a variety of sheds! The ground frame hut was saved and I am led to believe it has gone to the East Somerset Railway at Cranmore.

The deep cutting east of the station has been filled in for many years. The village won a major battle in 1983 to prevent a stretch between Brent Road in Cossington and the A39 being infilled with industrial waste, I am glad to say. A leachate pipe was laid a few years ago from the disused Cossington tip under the track bed towards Bawdrip, which has meant that the track-bed is still well defined in the deep cutting south-west of the village. *(Date: 10 June 1985.)*

141
Bawdrip Halt (182 ST 342 397)

Bawdrip Halt opened in 1923. The station was built in the basic SR style of prefabricated concrete single platform and shelter. It came into being after pressure was put upon the railway company by the parish led by the vicar of the period.

Seen here are two shoppers who have returned by train from Bridgwater—note those hats! In the background behind the shelter is the village hall, which has often been mistaken for the booking hall and station building. In fact it was never attached to the station in any way. The station closed for passengers on 1 December 1952. *(Photo: Real Photographs. Date: circa 1932.)*

Only the village hall remains. However the line back from here to the A39 road bridge (S&D No 305) has been cleared by a local landowner for use as a gallop. The line beyond the trees in the foreground now forms a garden for a bungalow built on the formation between here and Bridge No 306. *(Date: 26 June 1985.)*

142
Bawdrip (A39)
(182 ST 328 394)

Johnson 0-4-4T No 58073 fitted with condensing apparatus, a legacy from working through the Metropolitan tunnels in the London area, is about to pass under the A39 road bridge with an Edington Junction to Bridgwater goods.

Note the fireman's casual stance in riding the footplate! Almost certainly it matched the speed of the train! *(Photo: Ivo Peters. Date: August 1953.)*

I waited at least forty minutes for the sun to appear before taking this photograph. The dramatic sky aids what might have otherwise been a singularly boring view!

Note Bawdrip Church standing out in the sunlight, also the pylons can be identified as those in the original. The main A39 road was straightened after the removal of the bridge, but the line formation can still be seen behind the hedgerow on the left. *(Date: 24 May 1985.)*

143
Bridgwater-Bristol Road (A38) (182 ST 307 384)

I would suspect many people remember staring at this bridge for hours on end, for this road into Bridgwater used to be the main holiday route to the south-west from the Midlands and the North. The resulting jams caused by traffic trying to get through the town were horrendous!

Seen here is Johnson 0-4-4T No 58073 hurrying over the A38 with her train from Bridgwater North to Edington. The embankment continued over the GW line and dropped at 1:72 to take the line towards Horsey crossing.

The beer advertisement is now a relic of the past as is the brick and tile industry in Bridgwater proffered by John Board & Co, whose sign is seen on the right. *(Photo: via Douglas Allen. Date: 1952.)*

The bridge has long since disappeared, the embankment towards Bridgwater (North) on the west side of the A38 was removed many years ago to make way for industrial development. However the embankment on the east side and the pillbox remained here until fairly recently, only being removed in the last three or four years or so. The traffic on the A38 is still busy, with the Wylds Road Trading Estate generating even more as can be seen here joining the main road. *(Date: 24 May 1985.)*

Map 36, 1904: Bridgwater (North)

As the map suggests, Bridgwater had a thriving brick and tile industry; sadly no longer the case today.

The line from Bridgwater to Edington was opened on 21 July 1890, being built by an independent company 'The Bridgwater Railway' and was never in law owned by the S&D. The station building was of local brick and had the appearance of an L&SWR design. It stood at right angles to the two-bay island platform, upon which an awning was built covering half its length.

The goods yard, complete with shed, had ample facilities to handle many commodities including bricks, tiles and cattle. A fairly large single road engine shed of brick construction was also built, together with a 50 ft turntable. The shed was not used to stable engines overnight after 1928.

Up until 1942 there was a 48-chain extension which swung through 180° to provide wharfage facilities on the bank of the River Parrett.

The map also shows the GWR docks branch which crossed the river via the 'Black Bridge' gaining access to Bridgwater Docks. This was a telescopic draw bridge whose design was ingenious and unusual —it now carries road traffic. When the branch to Edington was finally closed in 1954, a new spur was added from the S&D yard to connect it to the GWR docks branch.

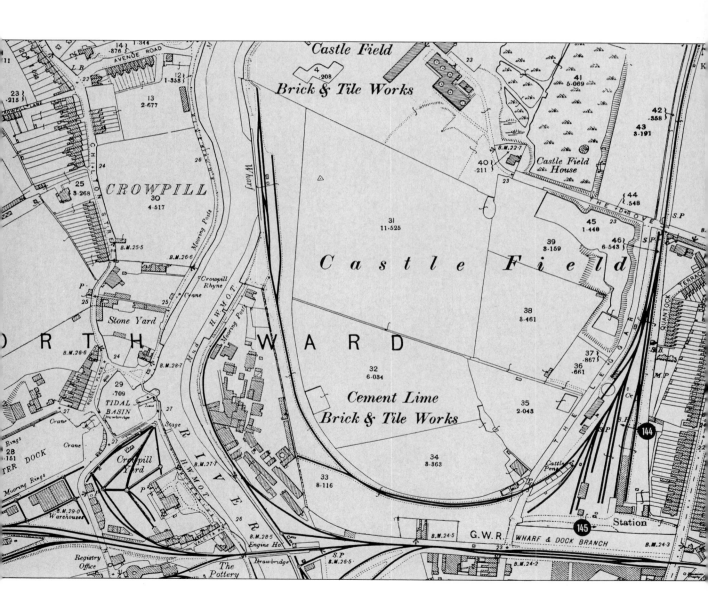

Bridgwater (North) (1)
(182 ST 304 375)

A '3F' 0-6-0 waits at Bridgwater (North) to take her train to Edington Junction, and the island platform with the awning covering half the length is seen to good advantage.

The station building ran at right angles to the buffer stops and is seen under the canopy. The station master's house is visible between the awning and the station sign in this photograph. *(Photo: Real Photographs. Date: 1951.)*

For many years, until recently the yard was used by BRS. Now the site is up for sale as small industrial units. The goods shed survived intact until July 1985 when it burnt down. The goods office survives in fair condition. The station building was demolished in August 1984 and the engine shed in December 1985. This photograph shows the ex-garage workshop of BRS. Note the terraced houses in the background and how the tree on the right has grown since 1951. *(Date: 24 May 1985.)*

Right Bridgwater (North) goods shed was destroyed by fire a little under a year after this picture was made. *(Date: 4 August 1984.)*

145
Bridgwater (North) (2)
(182 ST 303 374)

The station frontage was most attractive, built in red brick it had L&SWR influence. This commodious building housed a booking office and hall, two waiting rooms and lavatories.

Bridgwater (North) Station was a hive of activity on market days and it was not uncommon to see the odd bedstead, having been bought by one of the engine crews at market, travelling home on the back of the tender! *(Photo: Real Photographs. Date: 1935).*

I thought I would wait for better weather before taking a photograph of the station frontage, which I remembered as a boy. You can imagine my horror when I went to Bridgwater the day of Yeovilton Air Show on 4 August to collect a supply of film and saw the roof was off the building. My first thoughts were that BRS were refelting or repairing it, but investigation proved me wrong. So before I went to the air display I took this final shot of the building. Two or three days later it was no more. *(Date: 4 August 1984.)*

Left I subsequently photographed the culprit in the form of a mechanical digger, standing like a praying mantis, gloating over the rubble. *(Date: 8 August 1984.)*

146
Polsham Station
(182/183 ST 517 483)

There are very few photographs available of Polsham Station, which was on the Wells branch mid-way between Glastonbury and Wells.

The platform was 200 ft long and had a simple building providing basic facilities. A ground frame on the platform (seen in the foreground) controlled the crossing and a single siding. One goods train called per day to service the station. Latterly a large station master's house was incorporated on the platform next to the station building. This station closed on 29 October 1951 upon the closure of the branch. *(Photo: Real Photographs. Date: 1912.)*

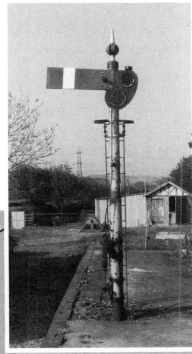

The station is now a private dwelling and sports various L&SWR railway artefacts, but the signal, **left**, is definitely Great Western! The platform lavatory is still there, complete with coin-operated lock! *(Date: 7 May 1985.)*

147
Coxley (182/183 ST 528 438)

This rare photograph shows 0-4-4T No 1346 approaching Coxley and passing under Bridge No 289, with a Glastonbury to Wells push-and-pull train. This branch was little used in the latter days and one might have been the only passenger on many of the trains! *(Photo: H. C. Casserley. Date: 1937.)*

The land has had over thirty years to heal and provides little clue to its railway heritage. The shed on the right can be identified as can the river bridge on the left. The pillbox (centre top) was built in 1940 and therefore did not feature in the original photograph. *(Date: 7 May 1985.)*

Map 37, 1902: Wells (Priory Road)

It is hard to believe that this small cathedral city had three stations all within 30 chains of one another!

The Somerset Central was the first into Wells, the station opening on 15 March 1859, and until 1862 its broad gauge track was the line's eastern arm from Highbridge, prior to the Bruton extension being built.

The second arrival in 1862 was the East Somerset Railway from Witham, also of broad gauge, building its station east of Priory Road. Last on the scene was the Cheddar and Yatton Railway, entering the city at Tucker Street from Yatton in 1870 (seen as the GWR station), again of broad gauge. These two converted to standard gauge in 1874–5 (in line with the Somerset Central which had by then become a part of the S&D and standard or narrow gauge).

An agreement was reached between the S&D and the GWR,

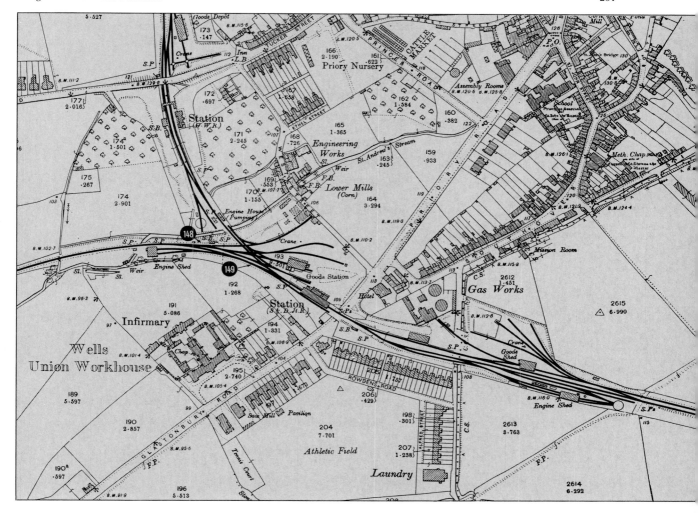

who by this date had absorbed the East Somerset & Cheddar companies. For a consideration of £400 per annum the GWR acquired the right to run trains over the 9 chains of S&D property. The short spur was completed to link the systems; the first passenger trains ran from Yatton to Witham from 1 January 1878. Thereafter the East Somerset station was only used for goods traffic.

Not until 56 years after the agreement had been signed was Priory Road station jointly used by S&D

and GWR trains. Trains ran from 1934–51 till closure of the S&D branch from Glastonbury. The S&D goods yard continued to be used by 'GWR' trains until 1964. The S&D branch carried few passengers, there often being only one or two people on a train!

One can see from the map how the systems were linked. The S&D's goods yard was spacious, provided with a shed and crane and a small two-road engine shed and a signal box on the western side. The station building had a covered roof.

Today the old S&D goods shed is the sole survivor of its railway system in Wells, apart from the nearby station master's house. Rubble from the old platform of Priory Road Station can be seen next to the goods shed. The platforms of the GWR station at Tucker Street are still there, together with the goods shed to the north. A new road has been constructed leading from Glastonbury/Priory Road over the old track-bed to a new housing development which is being built nearby.

148
Wells (Priory Road) (1)
(182/183 ST 544 453)

A nice view of Wells Priory Road
Station, showing the layout of the
goods shed and attendant yard. The
station building, minus its roof, is
seen middle right. The signal box
that controlled the goods yard and
crossing is seen on the left. The
GWR line ran in front of this and on
past Priory Road Station platform
towards Wells East and Witham.
*(Photo: David Milton. Date: 13 June
1960.)*

The yard in the foreground is owned
by Tincknells, agricultural engineers. The ramp is not of railway
heritage but was built for the load-
ing/unloading of flatbed lorries with
agricultural equipment. Note the
telegraph poles in this photograph
and also the old station master's
house seen in the background, next
to which is the surviving S&D goods
shed. *(Date: 5 June 1985.)*

149
Wells (Priory Road) (2)
(182/183 ST 545 453)

A fine study of the covered roof of the station platform, the goods shed to the left and the station master's house in the background. Note the level crossing over the road through the station which was the GWR line to Wells East and Witham. *(Photo: Real Photographs. Date: 1934.)*

The scene today. The goods shed survives as does the station master's house. Remains of Priory Road Station platform can just be made out in this photograph. A road has been built to service a new housing development near the old GWR Tucker Street Station and the adjacent playing fields. *(Date: 5 June 1985.)*

Appendix 1
Index for maps

1. Bath (Green Park) (1932) 12
2. Bath (1985) 14
3. Lyncombe Vale 27
4. Horsecombe Vale/Tucking Mill to Midford 1904–1930 33
5. Wellow 43
6. Paglinch Farm 50
7. Writhlington 52
8. Radstock (1904) 56
9. Radstock (1982) 57
10. Midsomer Norton 62
11. Chilcompton 69
12. Binegar 74
13. Masbury 80
14. Winsor Hill 87
15. Shepton Mallet 101
16. Evercreech New 111
17. Evercreech Junction (1902) 114
18. Evercreech Junction (1972) 115
19. Wyke Champflower 130
20. Cole 137
21. Wincanton 146
22. Templecombe (1903) 148
23. Templecombe (1978) 149
24. Henstridge 158
25. Sturminster Newton 162
26. Blandford Forum 173
27. Broadstone 185
28. Holes Bay & Poole 189
29. Branksome 191
30. Bournemouth West 194
31. Glastonbury 200
32. Edington 216
33. Highbridge 223
34. Highbridge Wharf 231
35. Burnham-on-Sea 235
36. Bridgwater (North) 245
37. Wells (1904) 251

Map Notes

1. The majority of the maps included to cover areas of specific interest and importance on the S&D System, are reproduced from the second and third editions of the Ordnance Survey 25in Series and their revision dates between 1902 and 1936.

2. By using these maps in conjunction with either the 1:50,000 Landranger or 1:25,000 Pathfinder Series when visiting the Line today, interesting comparisons can be made—any changes being all too apparent.

3. A few recent 1:2,500 scale maps have been reproduced to provide a stark contrast following the 'Then & Now' theme, Templecombe being the most obvious choice.

4. All maps featured are biased to Grid North.

Appendix 2
Land and structures still owned in 1985 by British Rail on the former Somerset and Dorset Line

Note: 1   Section 1 covers Chapters 1–6
        Section 2 covers Chapters 10–11
        Sections 3 & 4 cover Chapter 12
        Sections 5 & 6 cover Chapters 7–9

  2   All distances in Sections 1, 5 & 6 are given from Bath Junction

Section 1—Bath Green Park to Evercreech Junction

A bridge described as 'occ over or under' represents an 'Occupation Bridge', eg, a farm bridge or one permitting private access for occupiers of land bordering the line.

Property or land	Mileage M	C	Type	Comments
Bridge No 3	0	31	Under	Intersection with main line
Devonshire Tunnel (No 10)	1	32		
	1	52		
Viaduct No 16	3	21	Public Under	Tucking Mill Viaduct (8 spans)
Bridge No 17	3	55	Public Over	Long Arch Bridge
Viaduct No 18	3	72¼	Public Under	Midford Viaduct (8 spans)
	3	79¾		
Viaduct No 22	5	72½	Public Under	Wellow Viaduct (4 spans)
Bridge No 23	6	10½	Public Under	Abutments only
Bridge No 26	6	53	Public Over	Combe Hay Road
Bridge No 28	7	51	Public Over	Faulkland Road
Bridge No 29	8	02	Public Under	Abutments only
Viaduct No 31	8	37	Public Under	Home Farm Viaduct
	8	39		
Chilcompton Tunnel (No 49)	13	11¾		
	13	15		
Bridge No 51	13	51	Public Under	
Bridge No 52	13	61	Public Over	Chilcompton Road
Bridge No 53	14	00	Occ. Under	Chilcompton
Bridge No 59	15	17	Public Under	Abutments only
Bridge No 62	15	67	Public Under	North Abutment only
Bridge No 64	16	10	Public Under	Tellis Lane
Bridge No 68	17	33	Public Under	Gurney Slade Road
Bridge No 70	18	07	Public Over	Masbury Station
Bridge No 72	18	45	Public Under	Abutments only
Bridge No 73	18	51½	Occ. Under	
Viaduct No 75	19	27	Under	Ham Wood Viaduct (6 spans)
	19	30½		
Winsor Hill Tunnel (No 77)	19	52		
	19	63		
Bridge No 78	19	74	Public Under	Forum Lane
Viaduct No 81	20	25	Public Under	Bath Road Viaduct (6 spans)
	20	31		
Bridge No 85	21	16	Public Under	Abutments only
Bridge No 92	22	32	Public Over	Whitstone Lane
Viaduct No 95	22	75	Public Under	Prestleigh Viaduct (11 spans)
	23	0½		
Bridge No 101	24	23	Public Under	North Abutment only
Bridge No 102	24	46½	Public Under	South Abutment only
Viaduct No 105	25	12	Public Under	Pecking Mill Viaduct (6 spans)
	25	15		(part demolished)

Notes:

1 Additional land owned by British Rail is as follows:-
   a) Midford Station.   Let to S. Castens.

b) Double line formation from Writhlington Siding   Used by contractors' transport for coal reclamation at
   East of Bridge No 33 to Mill Road Industrial   Writhlington.
   Estate, Radstock.
c) Coal Yard, Chilcompton.   Let to private coal merchant.
d) Coal Yard and paddock, Binegar Station.   Let to private coal merchant.

2   Combe Down Tunnel was sold to Wessex Water Authority on 11 October 1982.

Section 2—Evercreech Junction to Highbridge

Property or land	Mileage		Type	Comments
	M	C		
Bridge No 247	2	44	Public Over	Pylle Woods
Bridge No 264	8	49	Public Over	Wells Road
Single Line Formation	8	62 ⎫		Including Cemetery Lane
	9	22 ⎭		Crossing
Bridge No 265	9	74	Public Over	Northload Bridge
Bridge No 266	10	26	Culvert Under	Dye House Lane
Double Line Formation*	10	25 ⎫		
	10	51 ⎭		
Bridge No 267A	10	51½	Culvert Outlying	
Bridge No 268	11	05	River Brue—under	
Bridge No 271E	18	74	Glastonbury Canal Outlying	Eastern Moor Bridge

Note:

*Glastonbury Station area extending to site of Glaston-   Most land and structures west of Glastonbury were sold
bury Canal (outlying) between Middle Drove (Bridge No   to Wessex Water Authority. BR still own 25.7 acres
267A) and down side of station yard, 38 chains in extent. covering the site of Highbridge (East) and the site of the
                                                           adjacent old works at the time of writing.

Section 3—Edington Junction to Bridgwater (North)

Property or land	Mileage		Type	Comments
	M	C		
Bridge No 299	1	75	Public Under	
Bridge No 300	2	09½	Public Over	Landshire Lane
Bridge No 301	2	58½	Public Over	Bell Lane
Bridge No 304	3	15½	Public Over	Brent Road, Cossington
Bridge No 305	3	48	Public Over	Glastonbury Road (A39)
Bridge No 306	4	14	Public Under	Bawdrip

Section 4—Glastonbury (1¼MP) to Wells

Property or land	Mileage (From 1¼MP)		Type	Comments
	M	C		
Bridge No 288	3	50½	River Under	River Sheppy Bridge
Bridge No 289	3	79½	Public Under	Burcott Road
Bridge No 289A	3	79½	River	River Sheppy Bridge

Section 5—Evercreech Junction to Templecombe

Property or land	Mileage		Type	Comments
	M	C		
Bridge No 115	27	69	Public Over	Bruton Road
Bridge No 116	28	03½	Public Under	Wyke Lane
Bridge No 117	28	31	Public Under	Demolished 9/84
Bridge No 119	28	42 ⎫	Public Under	Cole Viaduct—demolished
	28	44 ⎭		9/84
Bridge No 120	28	50	Public Under	Demolished 9/84
Bridge No 121	28	64½	Public Over	Pitcombe Road
Bridge No 122	28	79	Public Under	Pitcombe Viaduct
Bridge No 123	29	08	Public Under	
Bridge No 125	29	75	Public Under	
Bridge No 127	30	24	Public Over	Shepton Montague
Bridge No 133	32	55½	Public Under	
Bridge No 141	34	18½	Public Over	
Bridge No 146	35	37	Public Over	

Additional lands: Cole Station Yard

Section 6—Templecombe to Broadstone

Property or land	Mileage		Type	Comments
	M	C		
Bridge No 152	36	36	Public Over	Combe Throop Lane
Single Line Formation	36	36 ⎫		Templecombe (Lower)
	36	39¼ ⎭		
Bridge No 153	36	39¼	Over	South-Western main line
Bridge No 155	36	57	Public Over	
Bridge No 159	38	18	Public Over	Shaftesbury Road
Bridge No 160	38	29	Culvert Under	
Bridge No 161	38	78	Public Over	
Bridge No 163	41	16	Public Over	
Bridge No 169	42	07	Occ. Over	
Bridge No 172	43	59	Public Over	Sturminster Newton
Bridge No 176	45	35	Public Over	
Bridge No 180	46	46	Public Under	Shillingstone
Bridge No 182	47	57	Occ.	
Bridge No 184	48	36½	Public Under	
Bridge No 188	49	76½	Public Over	Stourpaine
Bridge No 219	58	03	Public Over	
Bridge No 220	58	30	Public Over	Bailey Gate Station
Bridge No 229	60	08	Public Over	
Bridge No 235	61	38	Public Over	Corfe Mullen Halt
Bridge No 236	61	44	Public Over	Lambs Green Lane
Bridge No 238	61	73	Public Over	

Note: between Bridge No 188 and No 217 all bridges, culverts, etc, were sold to Dorset County Council in 1972.

Appendix 3
Preserved Locomotives

A number of locomotives that ran over the line and actually spent time based at an S&D MPD have been preserved. This table does not include those that only spent very short periods of time on the line or made only an occasional trip.

*denotes locomotives in working condition
†named whilst in private ownership

I am grateful to Peter Smith for his help in compiling this list.

Class	Number	Name	Location
BR Standard '9F' 2-10-0	92220*	*Evening Star*	National Collection, York
BR Standard '9F' 2-10-0	92212		Gt. Central Railway, Loughborough
BR Standard '9F' 2-10-0	92203*†	*Black Prince*	E. Somerset Railway, Cranmore
BR Standard '5MT' 4-6-0	73050*†	*City of Peterborough*	Nene Valley Railway, Wansford
BR Standard '4MT' 4-6-0	75027*		Bluebell Line, Sheffield Park
Ex-S&D '7F' 2-8-0	53808		S&D Railway Trust, Washford
Ex-S&D '7F' 2-8-0	53809*†	*Beaumont*	Midland Railway Trust, Butterley
Ex-LMS '4F' 0-6-0	44422		N. Staffs. Railway Society, Cheddleton
Ex-GWR '22XX' 0-6-0	3205*		Severn Valley Railway, Bridgnorth
Ex-LMS '2MT' 2-6-2T	41241*		Keighley & Worth Valley Railway, Haworth

Appendix 4
Bibliography

The Somerset & Dorset Railway Robin Atthill, David & Charles

The Somerset & Dorset (An English Cross Country Railway) Ivo Peters, Oxford Publishing Co.

The Somerset & Dorset in the Fifties, Volumes 1 and 2, Ivo Peters, Oxford Publishing Co.

The Somerset & Dorset in the Sixties, Volumes 3 and 4, Ivo Peters, Oxford Publishing Co.

Historical Survey of The Somerset & Dorset Railway C. W. Judge and C. R. Potts, Oxford Publishing Co.

Steam on the Somerset & Dorset G. A. Richardson, D. Bradford Barton Ltd.

The Bridgwater Branch J. D. Harrison, Oakwood Press.

The Railways of Midford M. J. Arlett, Somerset & Dorset Railway Trust.

The Colour of Steam Vol 2 R. C. Riley, Atlantic.

The Picture History of the Somerset & Dorset Railway Robin Atthill, David & Charles.

Footplate over the Mendips P. W. Smith, Oxford Publishing Co.

Mendips Engineman P. W. Smith, Oxford Publishing Co.

The Railways & Tramways of Radstock Chris Handley, The Somerset & Dorset Railway Museum Trust.

Templecombe 1860–1985 Templecombe Station Working Committee.

Railways of the Southern Region Geoffrey Body, Patrick Stephens Ltd.

Railways in Wells R. Hayes and M. Shaw, 'HST'.

Modellers & Enthusiasts Guide to The Somerset & Dorset Line Brian Macdermott, Patrick Stephens Ltd.

An outline history of Bath (Green Park) Station M. J. Arlett, Somerset & Dorset Railway Trust/J. Sainsbury PLC.

Appendix 5
Acknowledgements

This task is always a pleasant duty, but full of pitfalls in case of omissions!

I should like to begin by thanking Keith & Kay Hardy of the Rhyme & Reason bookshop who 'launched' me in the first instance, secondly to Robin Atthill, who provided me with helpful information and photographs from his collection and was also responsible for putting me in touch with many other experts on the S&D. My thanks to Dave Milton, Ron Toop, David Cross, Will Locke, H. C. Casserley, Mrs A. O'Shea, Tony Wadley, Ian Matthews, Anne Scott, Douglas Allen, Dick Riley, Tony Richardson and Bill Vaughan-Jenkins, for supplying superb photographs and providing me with much information. Very special thanks to my friend, Ivo Peters, without whose help this book would not have been possible. My grateful thanks to Mike Arlett and Peter Smith, both of whom have helped me a great deal—Mike for assistance in choosing various photographs and for supplying me with a mass of information, also accompanying me on forays—Peter, whose similar help in the southern part was equally invaluable, and for the Foreword he kindly consented to write. In addition, Mike and Peter were kind enough to read through my manuscript. My thanks to Donald Beale, a splendid gentleman in his 84th year, for revisiting Branksome and Bournemouth West with Peter Smith and me.

My thanks also to Messrs Stothert & Pitt, Engineers, Bath, who made a special effort in providing a crane, enabling me to photograph Bath Sheds, also to Messrs Showerings and Messrs Tachograph Services at Shepton Mallet for providing the equivalent! To Val and Keith Nash at Evercreech Junction for their wonderful response in helping to recreate the footbridge by lending me their forklift truck!! My thanks to the Somerset County Records Office and Bridgwater Reference Library, whose long-suffering staff have endured hours of photocopying maps, to Messrs Humberts, Taunton & Messrs Cooper & Tanner, Glastonbury, for supplying further maps, also to Wansdyke District Council for their help in this respect and to Plessey Marine at Templecombe for allowing me to photograph from their site. I am also indebted to Paul Dye and David Fleming of the British Rail Property Board for their help in supplying very useful information regarding structures and lands still owned and maintained by BR—my grateful thanks.

I would like to thank the many landowners who allowed me to photograph from their land and many other people, including ex-S&D railwaymen, for allowing me to photograph from their property—Wilfrid Couling, Norman Down and Archie Attwell—to name but a few.

I am also grateful to Dr Peter Cattermole and Mike Palmer of the Somerset & Dorset Trust for their help in being able to supply me with vital information, sometimes of an obscure nature!!

Finally I would like to thank Jenny, my long-suffering wife, who typed through many nights and weekends and gave up the occasional day's 'holiday' to trudge three paces behind me carrying the cameras, tripods, maps, reference books, thermos—also my children, Kate, Nick and Suzannah, who never carried out their threat to abandon me on one of many disused railway platforms!

Appendix 6
The Somerset & Dorset Railway Trust

The Trust started as the S&D Railway Circle in 1966 with the prime aim of collecting and circulating information about the S&DJR. From 1969 to 1975 the Trust leased Radstock North Station, engine shed and yard, and housed a working railway museum. Upon expiry of the lease in 1975, the Trust moved to Washford on the West Somerset Railway, reopening that station in 1977.

Restoration work is undertaken at Washford, the chief project being the Trust's own locomotive S&D '7F' 2-8-0 No 53808 (S&D No 88) built in 1925 by Robert Stephenson & Co Ltd to a Fowler design. At the time of writing plans are well advanced in securing the services of professional restorers to enable 'No 88' to return to steam as soon as possible.

The Trust has also recreated a full-size replica of Midford signal box lever frame at Washford and has many other S&D relics of interest. It also has extensive archive material including many photographs and publishes a bi-monthly journal for its well-subscribed membership, which is packed with interesting information. The Trust museum is open most weekends and is worth a visit.

The Trust has also a large modelling fraternity and puts on an annual exhibition at Edington Village Hall, near Bridgwater.

The Somerset & Dorset Railway Trust Secretary is:

M. J. Palmer
The Haven
Chandlers Lane
Edington
Bridgwater
Somerset.

Appendix 7
Technical notes

The specifications of the equipment was as follows:-

Camera bodies Minolta XGM
Lens 1 MD Zoom Rokkor   28–85 mm f 3.5–f 4.5
     2 MD Rokkor   50 mm   f 1.7
     3 MD Rokkor   50 mm   f 2

Filters
Cokin System 'P' Series   Yellow + 1.5
                          Orange + 1
                          Green + 2⅔

Screw Filters
Sun   ⎫   Yellow + 1.5 55 mm.
Hoya ⎭   Skylight 1B
Sun   ⎫   Yellow   49 mm.
Hoya ⎭   Skylight 1A

Tripod
Kenlock 3000 SQB

Ancillary equipment
Minolta Auto Winder
Minolta Electronic Shutter Release Remote Cord S
20' Pneumatic Shutter Release

Photographic printing by: Quantock Photocrafts and P. J. Dibley, Rowford Lodge, Cheddon Fitzpaine, Nr Taunton, Somerset.

Film:
Black & White: Ilford FP 4, & PAN F
Colour: Kodak Vericolor III (print), Kodachrome 64 (transparencies).
The format used for facsimile photographs had to be 35 mm for practical reasons.

Appendix 8

MAPS TO SHOW THE LOCATION OF PHOTOGRAPHS NOT SHOWN ON MAPS IN MAIN TEXT.

Map no.	Photograph no.	Location	Map date	Map no.	Photograph no.	Location	Map date
1	10	Devonshire Bank, Bath	1932	17	108	Spetisbury (Spettisbury)	1901
2	22, 23	Lower Twinhoe	1904/1931	18	109	Bailey Gate	1936
3	28	Wellow Valley	1929	19	110, 111	Bailey Gate Crossing/Corfe Mullen Junction	1901
4	29	Shoscombe & Single Hill	1932	20	117	Pylle	1903
5	41, 42	Chilcompton Tunnel	1903	21	118	West Pennard	1904
6	45	Moorewood	1903	22	124	Ashcott	1904
7	46	Milepost 16 (near Binegar)	1903	23	125	Shapwick	1904
8	67	Cannard's Grave	1904	24	128	Huntspill Crossing	1904
9	68	Prestleigh Viaduct	1932	25	129, 130	Bason Bridge	1904
10	84, 85, 86	Shepton Montague	1903	26	139, 140	Cossington/Board's Siding	1904
11	87	Verrington, near Wincanton	1903	27	141	Bawdrip	1904/1923
12	97	Stalbridge	1903	28	142	Bath Road, Bawdrip	1904
13	101	Shillingstone	1901	29	143	Bristol Road, Bridgwater	1930
14	102	Cliff Bridge	1901	30	146	Polsham	1904
15	103	Stourpaine & Durweston	1901/1928	31	147	Coxley Wick	1904
16	107	Charlton Marshall	1929				

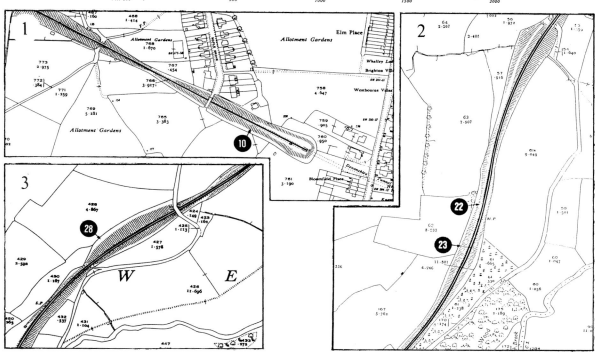

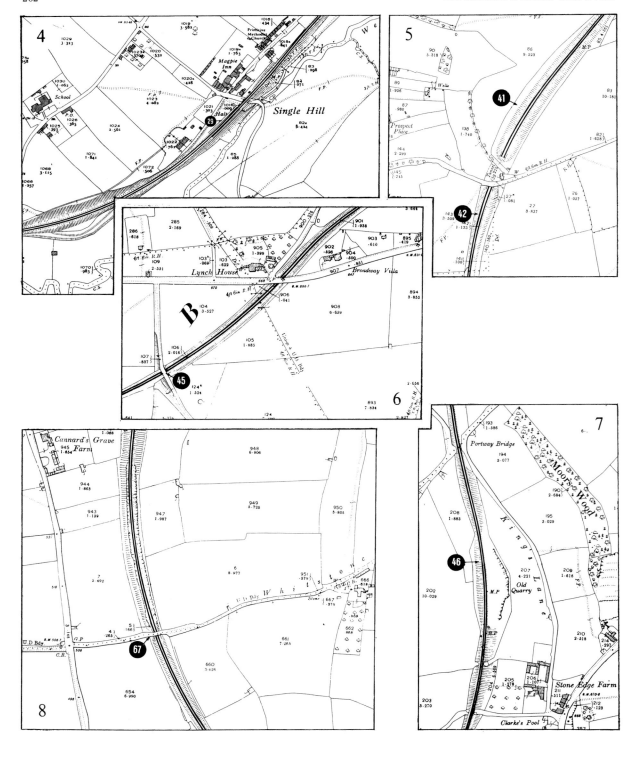

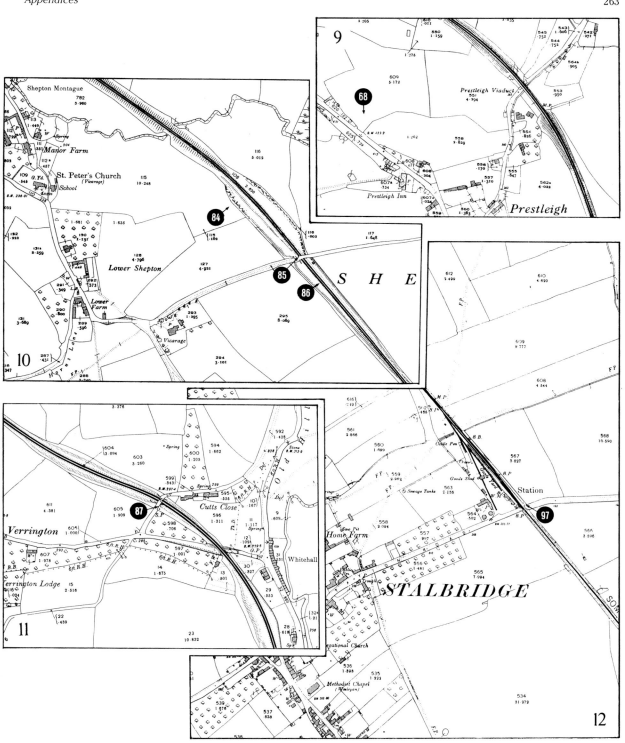

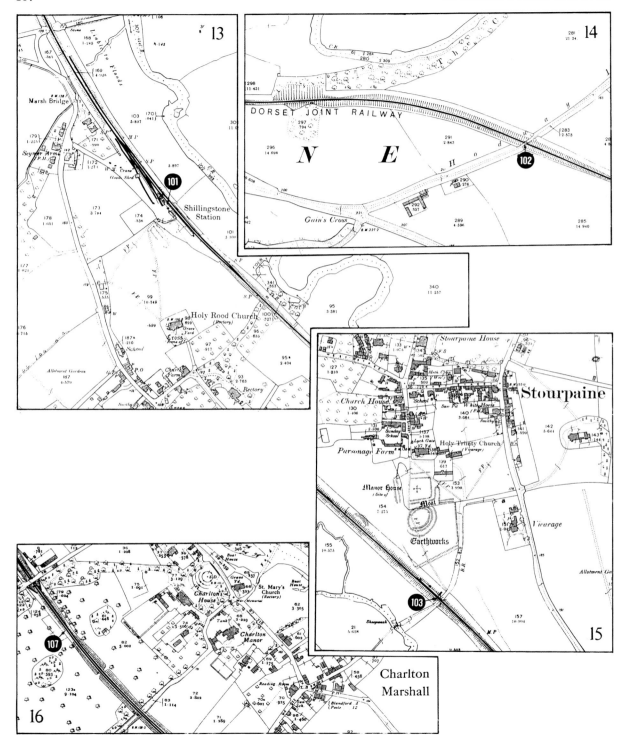

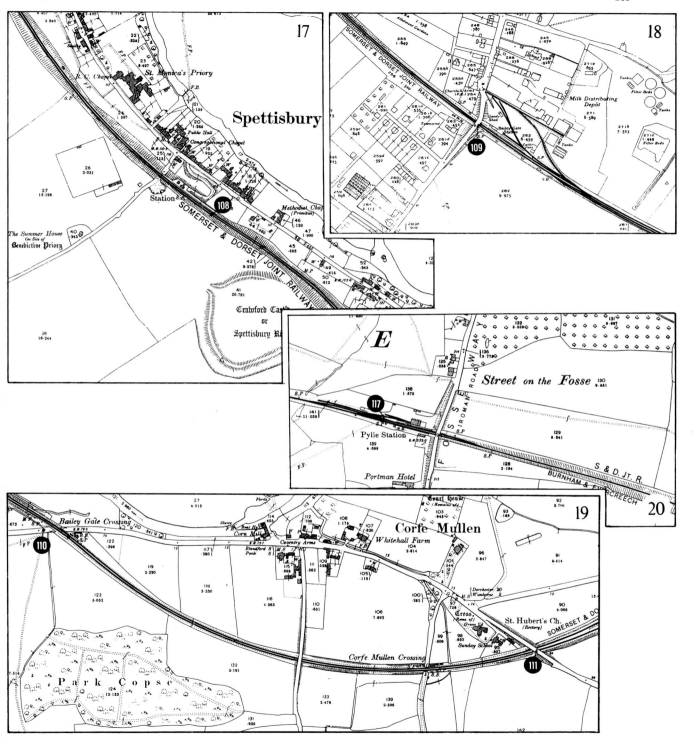

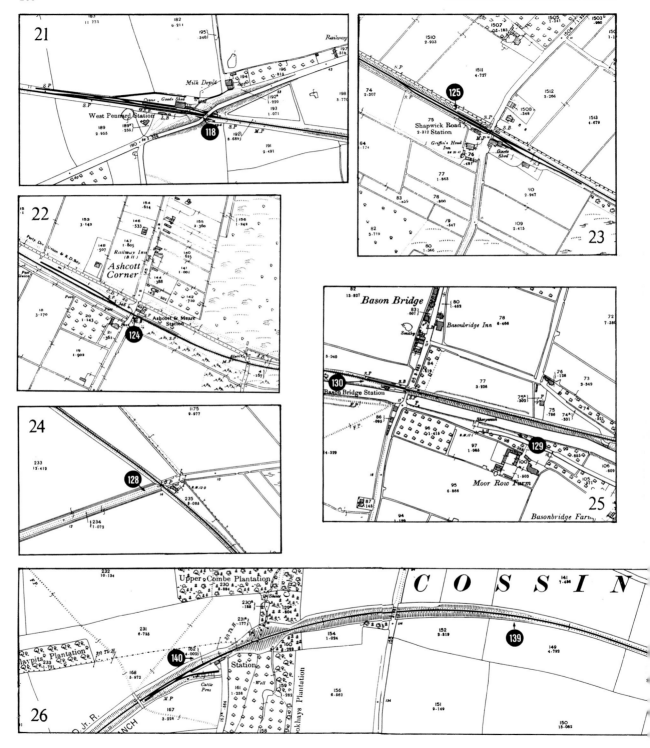

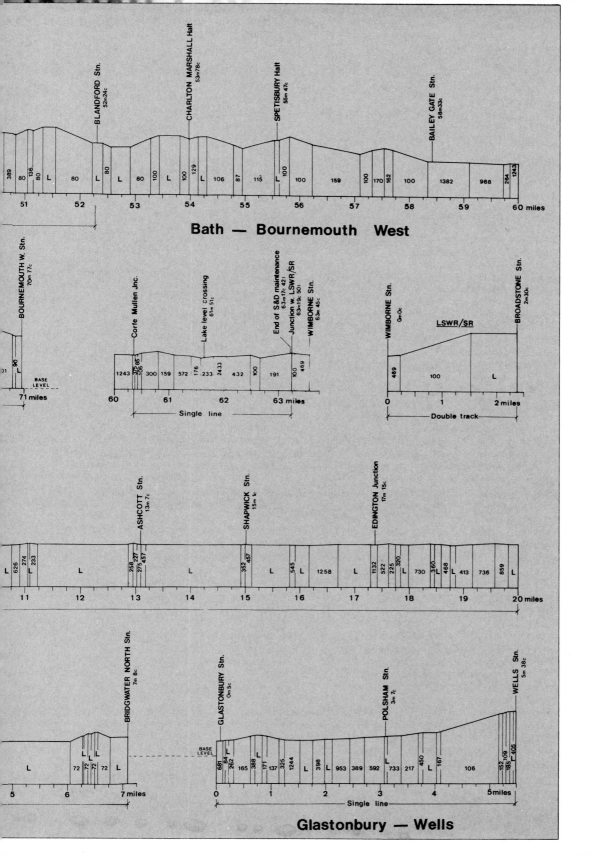

Bath — Bournemouth West

Glastonbury — Wells

A gentle reminder

Most of the 'Somerset & Dorset' is now privately owned farmland and therefore it is important to remember the 'Country Code' if exploring the route of the old line. It is a matter of common courtesy to obtain permission from local landowners before forays are made across land where there are no public footpaths, especially where livestock and crops are concerned, to keep dogs under control and to close all gates.

Many former stations are now private dwellings and therefore the privacy of householders should be respected. It is not uncommon for 'enthusiasts' to walk across somebody's front garden, which once might have been the track-bed between platforms, totally oblivious to any signs that state 'Private Property – Keep Out!' The natives are usually very friendly if approached in the correct manner! Do not forget that if the line were still operated by BR they would not take kindly to 'trespass.'

The Countryside Commission have published a useful booklet entitled 'Out in the Country' which is available, free of charge, through public libraries. It clearly states one's rights of way as well as the 'Do's and Don't's' of the countryside.

The basic rules of the 'Country Code':
1. Guard against all risk of fire
2. Fasten all gates
3. Keep dogs under control
4. Keep to public footpaths across farmland
5. Use gates and stiles to cross fences, hedges and walls
6. Leave livestock, crops and machinery alone
7. Take your litter home
8. Help to keep all water clean
9. Protect wildlife, plants and trees
10. Take special care on country roads
11. Make no unnecessary noise

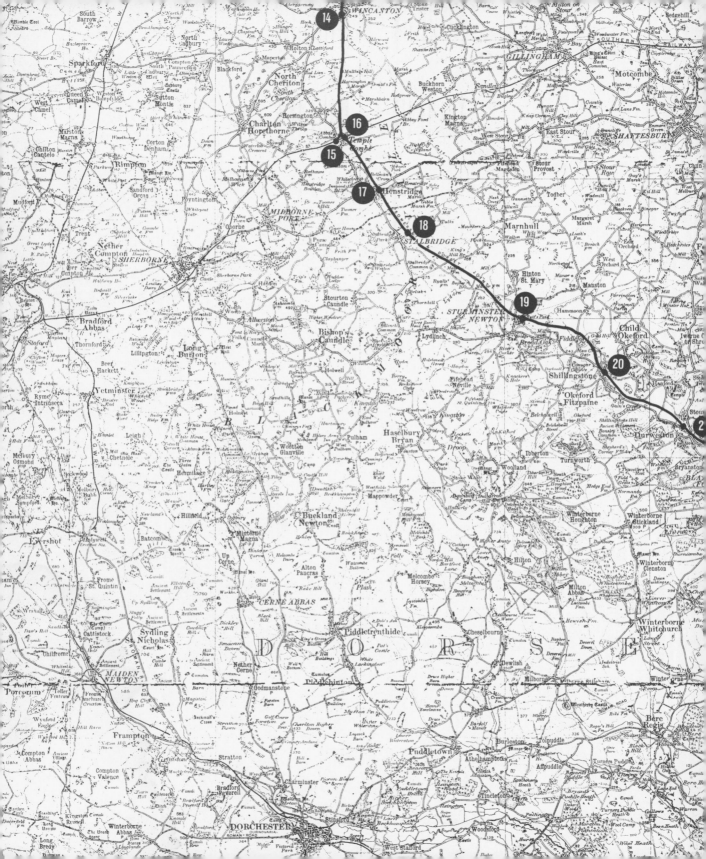

COMING HOME

Jack McDevitt titles published by Headline:

The Academy (Priscilla Hutchins) Novels
The Engines of God
Deepsix
Chindi
Omega
Odyssey
Cauldron
Starhawk

The Alex Benedict Novels
A Talent For War
Polaris
Seeker
The Devil's Eye
Echo
Firebird
Coming Home